Social Studies Curriculum

in

Perspective

Social Studies Curriculum

in

Perspective

a conceptual analysis

Gary Wehlage
University of Wisconsin

Eugene M. Anderson
University of Minnesota

PRENTICE-HALL, INC., ENGLEWOOD CLIFFS, NEW JERSEY

ISBN: 0-13-818823-8

Library of Congress Catalog Card Number: 79-176404

PRINTED IN THE UNITED STATES OF AMERICA

10 9 8 7 6 5 4 3 2 1

Prentice-Hall International, Inc., LONDON
Prentice-Hall of Australia, Pty. Ltd., SYDNEY
Prentice-Hall of Canada, Ltd., TORONTO
Prentice-Hall of India Private Limited, NEW DELHI
Prentice-Hall of Japan, Inc., TOKYO

To our wives
Nancy and Judy

Contents

Preface

Both universities and public schools of this country are making a fundamental reexamination of the purpose and meaning of their efforts. In the universities, the various disciplines of history and social science have seen the development of "radicals" who have challenged the traditional conceptions of research and knowledge. In addition, more conventional historians and social scientists have found it necessary and valuable to momentarily divert themselves from their usual research tasks in an effort to clarify and justify the methods and goals of their work. In elementary and secondary education the "free school" and "open classroom" movements can be seen as basic reevaluations of the goals of education. Questions are being raised concerning the extent to which schools should provide instruction in traditional subject matter as opposed to instruction aimed at the personal development of the individual. Also the traditional socialization and citizenship functions of the school are increasingly under attack by those who want students to acquire skills for social action.

In view of the reassessment that is taking place both in university disciplines and the public school curricula, the authors see the need for a basic treatment of the nature of social studies curriculum. We are offering a conceptual analysis of the most fundamental aspects of knowledge and curriculum. Our analysis attempts to provide a broad and balanced view of the various perspectives from which curriculum can be conceived. We hope that the depth and style of our work will encourage others to develop more systematic and careful analyses of the conceptual problems inherent in curriculum and instruction.

This book has been written for all who develop and teach social studies because we believe that there has been and continues to be a general need for a better understanding of the most fundamental issues underlying social studies curriculum. Different audiences, however, may find various parts of the book more or less relevant to their needs. The entire volume should be of interest to curriculum innovators and graduate students in social studies education at both the elementary and secondary level. Chapters 1 and 3, and particular sections of the chapters on concepts and generalizations are appropriate as supplementary materials in undergraduate methods courses. We also hope that the book will have a wide audience among general curriculum theorists and philosophers of science and social science because we believe that much of our analysis is applicable to the subject matter areas on which they focus.

The authors are indebted to several people who have directly or indirectly contributed to the development of this essay. Our thanks to Professors Lawrence E. Metcalf, C. Benjamin Cox, and Kenneth B. Henderson for helping us become aware of the need for conceptual analysis of social studies curriculum. In addition we wish to express our appreciation to John Palmer, Fred Newmann, and Michael Apple for their helpful criticisms during the preparation of this book. Believing that we are not wholly a product of our environment, we assume some of the responsibility for any inadequacies in our thinking.

Social Studies Curriculum
in
Perspective

Social Studies
Curriculum

1

Introduction

In June, 1970, a conference sponsored by the Social Science Education Consortium was held to discuss the future direction of social studies curriculum. One of the participants, John DeCecco, made a number of suggestions regarding the changes he saw ahead for the field. One of his main points was that social change is now so rapid that professionals can no longer argue that a body of basic knowledge must be taught to youth. He argued that the notion of national curricula for the social studies should be rejected in favor of developing local materials that would respond to local conditions. The emphasis should be on active civic involvement of students in decision making for their school and community. The belief held by many scholars—that there are inherent knowledge structures in the various disciplines—DeCecco declared to be a fantasy. There are many different ways, he maintained, of organizing information that can be useful to students, and educators ought to be willing to let students become partners in the business of scholarly inquiry. DeCecco concluded his remarks with the judgment that

> the heart of civic education does not lie in the subject matter of social studies courses, in curricular materials produced in university research and development centers, in the "structure of knowledge" of the social sciences, in new instructional methods for promoting "discovery," "problem-solving," and "inquiry," or even in field trips and community surveys which still confine the student to the role of passive observer and intruder. The new civic education can and will occur only as the school and community help the student consciously distinguish and exercise options for rendering school-community services which transform narrow private lives into liberal civic lives.[1]

The authors of this book find DeCecco's position to be interesting and hopeful in some respects. It suggests a level of personal involvement on the part of students that could be inherently interesting to them, and at the same time be preparatory to responsible sociopolitical behavior. On the other hand, this view of curriculum could signify a new educational fad based on shallow experiences masquerading under the cliché of "relevance." In today's conflict ridden society, it may be that curriculum simply will develop along the path of least resistance by responding to the often expressed desire of students to "get involved." In short, we are encouraged but also wish to warn against possible educational excesses. Thus, for DeCecco to say that knowledge structures are a fantasy, that university research and development can not produce useful national curricula, that because of rapid social change there is no core of knowledge necessary for students to know, and for him to suggest that youth are just as capable as scholars in thinking of useful ways to construe knowledge will, we fear, be interpreted by many to mean that "knowledge is dead"—that there is no need to engage in reflective, intellectual activities.

There has, of course, been a tendency in education for fads to develop when a particular viewpoint or objective becomes popularized. For example, the post-sputnik craze for teaching the "hard" disciplines *qua* disciplines resulted in curricula that in many cases had the life squeezed out of them. It could well be that we are now in a period of reaction against the kind of intense discipline-oriented social studies that stressed inquiry and structure, and in a sense sought to make students into little league historians, economists, and so on. To the extent that this view of curriculum was narrow, rigid, and without significance to many stu-

---

[1] John P. DeCecco, "Curriculum For the Seventies: Social Science or Civic Education?" Paper delivered June 12, 1970, at Phipps Conference Center, Denver University, Denver, Colorado, sponsored by Social Science Education Consortium, Inc.

dents, DeCecco's plea for a new set of priorities is understandable and quite appropriate. On the other hand, we hope the field will not be swept by a new fad characterized by curricula built in an intellectual vacuum.

The primary thrust of this book is designed to clarify the nature of the knowledge that can be employed in developing social studies content.[2] Our intention is to make distinctions that will be helpful in deciding what knowledge, available to the teacher and student, is most useful and relevant to them. The point of our analysis is to suggest implications for social studies curriculum.

Some Trends in the Social Studies Curriculum

It may be helpful to get some background on what has happened to the social studies curriculum in terms of assumptions about the knowledge to be taught; i.e., what claims of significance and value have been made for the social studies. Without going into detail on the development of the field, some dominant trends can be noted to indicate changes in rationale and content.

Before 1890, social studies meant primarily the teaching of history. History as a discipline was said to be valuable for a variety of reasons (some of which are still cited today): it served as moral and religious training, it afforded training for citizenship and inspired patriotism, and it strengthened the mind through the mental discipline provided by the subject matter.

From 1890 to 1920, there were several national committees which attempted to clarify the objectives for teaching social studies. History still dominated the picture, but the utilitarian function of this discipline was shifting slightly and the rationale was becoming more sophisticated. Basically, the contention was that history made people socially intelligent, developed a sense of historical mindedness, and provided information that would explain the present. The Committee of Seven of the American Historical Association argued that history was beneficial because it led to an understanding of cause and effect, it provided training in how to obtain and use facts, it developed the scientific habit of mind, and all this strengthened and disciplined the mind.

The rationale for social studies education was beginning in the early part of the twentieth century to be couched more in terms of training

2 We are using the term knowledge to include "knowing that" something is the case and also the knowledge that comes from "knowing how" to do something. See Gilbert Ryle, *The Concept of Mind* (London: Hutchinson University Library, 1949), chap. 2; also see Jane Roland Martin, "On the Reduction of 'Knowing That' To 'Knowing How'" in B. O. Smith and R. H. Ennis, eds., *Language and Concepts in Education* (Chicago: Rand McNally, 1961).

for citizenship. There was an increasing emphasis on meeting the needs of a society that was becoming industrialized and urbanized. The National Education Association's Commission on the Reorganization of Secondary Education enunciated the famous Seven Cardinal Principles: health, command of the fundamental processes, worthy home membership, vocation, citizenship, worthy use of leisure, and ethical character. The Commission's Committee for the Social Studies declared a need to broaden the content of the curriculum. Geography and civics were suggested as new areas of emphasis for junior high schools, and senior highs should concentrate more on the social sciences through a course in problems of democracy. This course could draw upon the disciplines in dealing with various social, economic, and political problems.

By the 1930s and 1940s, the American Historical Association was deeply involved in trying to clarify the nature of social studies education. Charles Beard was primarily responsible for the first of a series produced by the Commission on the Social Studies. Beard wrote that the purpose of social studies is "the creation of rich, many sided personalities, equipped with practical knowledge and inspired by ideas so that they can make their way and fulfill their mission in a changing society which is part of a world complex." [3] Knowledge from history and the social sciences cannot, according to Beard, ignore considerations of social value. Social education should consciously work to strengthen democratic institutions, make clear how these institutions work, point out defects in them, and promote a critical awareness among the citizenry.

In his own book, *The Nature of the Social Sciences,* Beard argued that subject matter ought to illuminate two considerations: "the good life for the individual and the social arrangements which are compatible with this good life and calculated to promote it." [4] In his writing he argued for a curriculum of social criticism which clarified the concept of the good life, and an empirical investigation into the means for achieving this end. The various disciplines fulfilled this latter requirement.

During the '30s and '40s there was also a counter movement taking place. Curriculum was developed around the concept of "education for life adjustment." [5] This approach to curriculum did not rely on the formal disciplines, but rather looked to the problems of living in a modern technological society for the focus of its attention. The main

---

[3] Charles A. Beard, *A Charter for the Social Sciences* (New York: Charles Scribner's Sons, 1934), pp. 96-97.

[4] Charles A. Beard, *The Nature of the Social Sciences* (New York: Charles Scribner's Sons, 1934), p. 188.

[5] U.S. Department of Health, Education, and Welfare, Office of Education, *Life Adjustment for Every American Youth,* Office of Education Bulletin 1951, No. 22. (Washington, D.C.: U.S. Government Printing Office, 1951.)

question for social studies curriculum was, "What are the needs of young people maturing in contemporary society?" Once these needs have been identified, it is possible to prescribe content and objectives. In other words, content and objectives are unknown until a set of needs have been established.

Social education, according to the life adjustment approach, did not assume that there were bodies of knowledge from the disciplines that must be taught. Instead, students learned such personal and social skills as being good family members, making wise vocational choices, and managing one's money intelligently. Curriculum units were concerned with problems of group living and understanding the social and occupational roles of the community. The skills learned in the life adjustment curriculum were more specific and directly applicable than those gained from the disciplines. Students were taught to read newspapers, advertisements, labels, and the fine print in contracts. They had experiences in writing letters and filling out job applications. The skills learned in the life adjustment curriculum were those that students most likely would use and benefit from in daily life. They are not the abstract skills associated with history and the social sciences such as recognizing causal factors and explaining the present by reference to the past.

The process involved in a life adjustment curriculum is based on direct experience. The assumption is that students learn not from teacher-conceived and -controlled curriculum, but rather that students learn from a curriculum in which they function as group members responsible for their own decisions. Life adjustment curriculum is designed to provide experiences in democratic living. This approach assumes that an ability to participate effectively in group situations is a basic skill that everyone needs to learn. Life adjustment is general education suited to all students regardless of intellectual ability, social class, or future vocational career.

The specifics of this curriculum approach need not be specified in advance, and considerable teacher-pupil planning is implied. Students help in determining what is studied, how it is studied, and even participate in the evaluation process. Life adjustment curriculum was, and (to the extent that it still guides curriculum development) *is* a way of responding to real life needs and problems. The disciplines may have useful knowledge that can be employed in dealing with these situations, but one does not begin with a discipline and then devise ways of getting students to learn it under the assumption that it will be useful at some point in the future, or that the discipline is somehow essential to the healthy development of the individual.

There was, of course, a harsh reaction against the life adjustment curriculum in the post-sputnik era. Actually, severe criticism had been leveled against it by people like Arthur Bestor during the 1950s.[6] Essentially the criticism was aimed at what was considered the "softness" of this approach. School was seen by the critics as a place where intellectual development should take place, and the way to do this was by grappling with those disciplines which were the result of man's most systematic and productive thought. It was argued that social and civic development could not take place without a basic intellectual development. Thus, school should deal with subjects that have disciplines like physics, mathematics, economics, and so on. In contrast with this position, life adjustment curriculum is characterized by projects and problems which, it was claimed, resulted in a hodgepodge that did not require one to learn a disciplined way of thinking. Social studies becomes "social stew" instead of history, sociology, and economics.

During the 1960s the theme was generally one of returning to the disciplines in one way or another. The tone was set by Jerome Bruner in his now classic work, *The Process of Education*. One of the themes Bruner stressed was that the heart of a curriculum should be based on the structure of a discipline. The teaching-learning process is enhanced by structure because it provides a systematic way to organize facts. Structure provides understanding, retention, and transfer by allowing students to see relationships among facts. In Bruner's words, "Grasping the structure of a subject is understanding it in a way that permits many other things to be related to it meaningfully. To learn structure, in short, is to learn how things are related." [7]

The search for the structure or structures on which to build social studies curriculum has taken several directions. Probably the most widespread approach has been to identify concepts and generalizations that can provide a framework around which to build specific content for instruction.

The Social Studies Curriculum Center at Syracuse University, for example, identified thirty-four concepts which are said to be interdisciplinary and suitable for developing a K-12 curriculum.[8] The concepts range across the various disciplines and deal with methodology as well as values. Similar to this is the Wisconsin Conceptual Framework which offers what are believed to be the major concepts within the disciplines of history, political science, anthropology, sociology, economics, and geography.[9] The objective of this framework is to provide a conceptual basis

---

[6] Arthur Bestor, *Educational Wastelands* (Urbana: University of Illinois Press, 1953).

[7] Jerome Bruner, *The Process of Education* (Cambridge, Mass.: Harvard University Press, 1962), p. 7.

[8] Roy A. Price, et al., *Major Concepts for the Social Studies*, Social Studies Curriculum Center (Syracuse, N.Y.: Syracuse University Press, 1965).

[9] *A Conceptual Framework for the Social Studies in Wisconsin Schools*, Department of Public Instruction, Madison, Wisconsin, 1964.

for a spiral curriculum that is said to broaden and deepen the knowledge students acquire as they progress through the grades.

Another curriculum that has relied heavily on a specific set of concepts was developed at Carnegie-Mellon University by Edwin Fenton. His approach was to identify what he calls "analytical" and "procedural" concepts. Analytical concepts are taken from political science, economics, and sociology: the basic concepts are leadership, decision making, ideology, scarcity, resources, price, role, status, and norms. These concepts serve as the nucleus for questions about a government, an economy, and a society. The analytical questions are the vehicles for hypothesis testing. To engage in this operation students must acquire procedural concepts such as hypothesis, fact, data, evidence, frame of reference, generalizations, theory, and concept.[10] By using evidence obtained through concepts, hypotheses are tested and students learn to engage in a kind of inquiry employed by professionals in the disciplines.

While concepts have received considerable attention as the basic building element for curriculum, there has also been an attempt to identify fundamental generalizations which are descriptive of regularities in human behavior. The California Study, for example, had representatives of each social science indicate what knowledge their particular discipline had to offer with respect to social studies education.[11] As in the case of several conceptual frameworks, the purpose was to provide a foundation for curriculum development by teachers and curriculum specialists. The result of the study was a synthesis of various discipline-centered generalizations into eighteen overarching statements reflecting the recurring ideas found in the various generalizations.

Another attempt to develop a framework for curriculum through a set of generalizations is found in the work of Paul Hanna and Associates at Stanford.[12] Their approach was to identify ten basic human activities and then to see which generalizations from the social sciences were applicable to them. During the course of their research more than 3,000 generalizations were identified. These were seen as a rich and authoritative source of knowledge around which a curriculum could be built.

There are a number of other curriculum efforts that focus on generalizations as the end pro⋅uct of inquiry. For example, Edwin Fenton wants students to arrive at generalizations as conclusions to the process of testing hypotheses. Fenton specifies the generalizations which are to

[10] Edwin Fenton, *Developing a New Curriculum: A Rationale for the Holt Social Studies Curriculum* (New York: Holt, Rinehart and Winston, Inc., 1967).
[11] State Curriculum Commission, *Social Studies Framework for the Public Schools of California* (Sacramento, Calif.: State Department of Education, 1962).
[12] Paul R. Hanna and John R. Lee, "Content in the Social Studies," in *Social Studies in the Elementary Schools*, 32nd Yearbook of the National Council for the Social Studies (Washington, D.C.: The Council, 1962).

be developed by students through inquiry, however he places less importance on them in comparison with the California Study or Paul Hanna's work. Fenton is more concerned with having students go through the process that leads to a generalization. As he sees it, there is danger in using lists of generalizations as the basis of curriculum. "Lists of generalizations are inert. They become ends in themselves, tempting teachers to choose generalizations from a list, smorgasbord-fashion, for their students, rather than means to an end."[13] Fenton's aim is to teach students the process by which they can arrive at generalizations.

In summary, the movement to base curriculum on concepts and generalizations is a response to the call for structure in the social studies. Clearly there is more than one way to define structure, but the concept has served to foster a general curriculum movement. To base curriculum on structure suggests the employment of scholars and scholarly knowledge in the creation of subject matter. Structure gives focus to what many people see as the central purpose of the schools—intellectual development. Those who have held this position in the past have traditionally looked to the disciplines for the raw materials upon which to build curriculum.

Although the 1960s found structure a popular theme in social studies education, there were, of course, a number of criticisms of this concept. Chief among these was the argument that no authoritative or reasonably final set of structural components had been found. Each scholar or group of curriculum developers seemed to be able to identify what they felt were the basic or major components. The result was a plethora of plausible structures each with its adherents. Yet none of them were able to show a clear superiority as the basis for the development of curriculum. Also some critics were doubting that students should be taught to think and act like historians, economists, and geographers. Fred M. Newmann, for example, pointed out that social scientists ordinarily do not ask questions such as: "Should a business man be able to charge all the traffic will bear?" Or, "When is it right to use violence to overthrow a government?"[14] These are important ethical questions that many young people might consider, and they are valuable in helping a student clarify his position on important social policies and controversies. However, ethical questions are not the heart of the various disciplines, and in fact, many social scientists wish to avoid them at all costs in attempting to produce objective knowledge.

[13] Edwin Fenton, *The New Social Studies* (New York: Holt, Rinehart and Winston, Inc., 1967), p. 13.
[14] Fred M. Newmann, "Questioning The Place of Social Science Disciplines In Education," in W. E. Gardner and F. A. Johnson, eds., *Social Studies in the Secondary Schools* (Boston: Allyn and Bacon, Inc., 1970), p. 119.

Newmann also suggests that basing curriculum on structures found in the various disciplines excludes experiences in nondisciplined ways of knowing which are also important. There are experiences with feelings, emotions, imagination, and fantasy. There are also a wide variety of skills that are not primarily intellectual—craft, art, athletics—that help to develop a person's sense of identity and competence. According to Newmann these are all important aspects of a person's educational development, but as he points out "the model of the scholar pursuing truth in his study or his laboratory obscures these dimensions of education." [15]

It may be that social studies will reject structure of the disciplines as a viable base for curriculum. If this rejection takes place, it will be in part at least the result of an inability to develop the concept in such a way that it is relevant to the need for competence in civic action. In part it will also have proved inadequate to meet the desires of students and teachers for a humanistic, people-centered education. Structure has generally been presented and interpreted as abstract knowledge that seems removed from the real concerns of people. Finally, structure has not appeared to meet the needs of students for personal development. Young people want to feel they can relate to other people, and that they are developing in social competence. They need to gain a sense of identity and a perspective on vocational choices. In general, the concept of structure of the disciplines has not been successful in meeting these needs. Except for a very few students who will become professionals in history or social science, the kind of education offered by a structure-based curriculum often is not seen as education for life. It is narrow vocational training imposed on everyone.

The disillusionment that has been expressed over structure is understandable in that too often it has become an end in itself. To learn a discipline, or at least to learn concepts and generalizations used by social scientists, has seemed rather meaningless to many, especially if the discipline is couched in terms of behavioral objectives unrelated to what are perceived as real problems for the individual or society. By an over zealous and narrow promotion of structure-based curriculum, social studies education may find itself undergoing a broad shift—a swing of the pendulum away from reflective analysis toward the active and emotional. The authors foresee an emphasis on such "relevant" experiences as sensitivity training, human relations, and sociopolitical action. We believe that this kind of shift in social education has some merit, that it ought to have a place in the schools, but at the same time we feel it would be unfortunate if this kind of curriculum resulted in a rejection

[15] Ibid., p. 119.

of reflective, rational, and analytical knowledge. To agree that it is important for students to gain a sense of identity, or to engage in meaningful civic activities should not be interpreted to mean that systematic intellectual activities including the use of disciplined based knowledge and process ought to be rejected from social education. What is needed is a relationship that balances systematic pursuit of knowledge, civic action, and personal development.

Three Logical Components of Knowledge

Before a balanced mode of curriculum can be achieved it is necessary to clarify the role that knowledge can legitimately play. It is clear to the authors that those who advocate teaching the structure of a discipline do have some insights into a kind of knowledge that can be useful. On the other hand, the authors believe that a curriculum designed to foster civic action and personal development also includes useful and important knowledge. In the succeeding chapters we hope to clarify the nature of this knowledge whether it comes from a formal discipline or whether it is derived from civic action or interpersonal activities. We believe an important contribution to social studies curriculum can be made through an analysis of the nature of basic logical aspects of knowledge. Our analysis is concerned with those logical components that are common not only to the various disciplines, but that are also fundamental to systematic thought and communication outside formal disciplines. A conceptual analysis of the type found in the following chapters is significant for those who would base their curriculum on structure, and it is equally important for those who would offer a problematic- or civic-oriented curriculum.

We contend there are three principal logical components which any social studies curriculum needs to have clarified if it is to provide meaningful knowledge. These components are *concepts, generalizations,* and *explanations.* (In terms of process, these elements become conceptualizing, generalizing, and explaining.) These logical components are universal in that they are basic to all communication about phenomena taking place in the world. For example, the physicist, economist, and the man on the street are each interested in offering and receiving explanations for certain events. Similarly, both professionals and laymen constantly employ concepts and generalizations in describing and evaluating the world around them. Even though these logical elements are commonplace in ordinary as well as professional language, the authors contend they are inadequately understood. This is apparent, we believe, in the work of those who have built social studies curricula around con-

cepts, generalizations, and the structures of disciplines. It is our contention that an analysis of concepts, generalizations, and explanations will
clarify their nature and thereby provide an intelligent basis from which
to choose and reject content for social studies curricula.

In the following chapters we make a number of distinctions that have
implications for choosing social studies content. A framework for these
distinctions is found in a theme that ties together our analysis of the
above mentioned logical components. This theme suggests that all knowledge consists of concepts, generalizations, and explanations, and that
knowledge can be conceived from an objective or subjective perspective.
On the one hand, knowledge can be developed through objective means
or methods (the goal of the sciences). Ordinarily historians and social
scientists are concerned with being objective in their research. On the
other hand, knowledge can be developed or perceived subjectively.
People have private insights, emotions, and unique reactions to the world
around them. Subjective knowledge is personal; objective knowledge is
public.

In formal terms, objective knowledge is that which exists in reality
independent of any person's perceptions. An objective view of knowledge sees reality as something independent of the mind, separate from
unique and personal perceptions of it. Objectivity is the result of intersubjectively observing and verifying reality. Individuals attempting to
be objective must focus on common meanings and data in the intersubjective process so that precise communications and observations can
be shared. In other words, the intersubjective process produces knowledge that is objective because it can be comprehended and examined by
a community sharing the same language and related meanings.

Subjective knowledge, on the other hand, exists as the result of unique
and personal perceptions of the world. A subjective view of knowledge
sees reality created by a unique mind. Subjectivity is the result of an
individual building his perceptions by focusing on what he sees as the
unique aspects of an object, event, or experience. For him, reality is
shaped by drawing on particular and peculiar insights and references
that mediate situations. Subjective views are the result of private language and meanings which are used to construe the world. Thus, each
person's unique background permits him to create a subjective view of
a situation.

The authors recognize that the distinctions between objective and subjective need qualifying if they are to be useful to people concerned with
curriculum development. First, it should be pointed out that objective
frameworks are subjectively held by those who use them. Scientists, for
example, have a number of assumptions, methods, and structures within
the scientific system to which they are committed. Scientists have a com-

mitment based on faith (at least in part) that the paraphernalia surrounding their enterprise will help them arrive at truth. Scientists have a very real emotional investment in the institution called science. Thomas Kuhn in *The Structure of Scientific Revolutions* points out that historically scientists have had a strong committment even to particular paradigms within their disciplines.[16] For instance, the Ptolemaic conception of the universe was adequate up to a point in describing and explaining the behavior of the planets. However, eventually it became cumbersome and unable to account for certain observed phenomena. Despite its inadequacies individuals retained the Ptolemaic theory rather than break their commitment and develop a new paradigm. Eventually, of course, the Copernican conception was successful in overthrowing its predecessor. Kuhn points out repeatedly the difficulty science has had in divesting itself of certain paradigms even in the face of considerable empirical and theoretical evidence to the contrary. The point to be made here is that any given objective framework, or more specific structure within it, can be objective only within the confines of a set of assumptions. This is to say that an objective framework is itself held subjectively. Ultimately one has faith that a particular framework provides truth.

This point has at least two significant implications for the arguments being presented here. First, the authors are *not* arguing that there is something "real" out there in the world which is objectively true, but rather that frameworks and paradigms serve to objectify and validate knowledge for those who operate within a system. Second, there can be many different objective frameworks and paradigms, and what is conventionally known as science or the scientific method is only one of these.

In order to clarify these two points, it may be useful to look at some examples of objective frameworks. The physicist operates with this kind of framework. More than most other disciplines, physics has been able to arrive at knowledge of considerable reliability through sets of precise operations and canons of evidence. A particular physicist might also have religious beliefs which permit him to hold objective knowledge about God and the nature of man. These two frameworks are quite different, but both can function objectively for an individual within their separate realms. Religion is objective to the extent that it permits a person to gain general insights, deal with experiences common to those operating within the system, and in general to communicate by means of a shared language. Any framework is objective to the extent that it permits a person to find some kind of validation outside himself for his experiences and knowledge.

Another example of objectivity is the kind of framework that a group

---

[16] Thomas S. Kuhn, *The Structure of Scientific Revolutions* (Chicago: The University of Chicago Press, 1970).

or public has created informally to deal with specific phenomena in a society. Thus as a group, racial bigots tend to create an objective framework within which to judge certain experiences and events. This kind of group has had common experiences with blacks and other minority groups. They know from real life experiences that black people are inferior. The deeply prejudiced person has a commitment to a framework that allows him to use evidence and communicate with others based on a common set of meanings. The group is able to develop and use generalizations: for example, blacks have a higher crime rate than whites, blacks on the average have a lower IQ than whites, blacks tend to earn less money than whites, and so on. The strength of these generalizations and the significance they hold comes in part from the fact that they are an aspect of a public knowledge. They have been verified and brought to conclusions within the confines of a particular group. It is difficult to challenge such knowledge because it has become objective by the standards of the group to which individuals have a subjective commitment.

What, if anything, is the difference between science as an objective framework and other subgroups or areas of society that also create objective frameworks? The key difference stems primarily from the deliberate and conscious effort of scientists to engage in an intersubjective examination of evidence, communications, and claims through the ordinary senses. By intersubjective is meant the cross-checking and demand for public verification that is built into the scientific process. Ideally, science demands that within its system every assumption, argument, and item of evidence must be scrutinized for adequacy. (Of course, this ideal is usually only approached and not achieved.) There are formalized techniques within the scientific system for guaranteeing that the intersubjective process is utilized. Other objective processes and frameworks also have ways of reviewing and examining knowledge, but none has as a canon of the framework itself that the intersubjective process takes place in a conscious and systematic way when treating empirical evidence. The system of science is not strangely dissimilar from ordinary intelligence and experience, but it is much more careful in the way it goes about objectifying what it calls knowledge.

The dichotomy between public and personal knowledge is in fact not always easy to make when confronting specific examples. The term knowledge is itself somewhat vague, and thus it may be more appropriate to think in terms of an objective-subjective continuum. It is clear there are many instances of objective knowledge (George Washington was the first President of the United States, the Japanese bombed Pearl Harbor, December 7, 1941, and John F. Kennedy was shot in Dallas, Texas), and it is also clear that everyone has his own peculiar way of construing the world (what one person sees as justice another sees as injustice, what produces rage in one person has no effect on another). However, it is also probably the case that someone's knowledge of, say, social class in contemporary America is a mixture of both objective and subjective views. Thus one's fund of knowledge may contain a large number of objective facts that have been verified through social science research methodology, but nevertheless the same person may have a number of views that are the result of his particular way of looking at the contemporary scene. None of us can permanently escape ourselves in looking at the world.

The authors believe the objective-subjective dichotomy (or continuum) to be a useful one for the field of social studies. In the natural sciences, for instance, this distinction would not be particularly helpful since these disciplines are almost totally committed to a search for objective knowledge. Over the centuries there has developed a set of methodological principles and rules designed to assist scientists in the discovery of objective facts and their relationships within the natural world. Modern science is inseparable from the concept of objectivity. On the other hand, the humanities and arts are closely allied with the concept of subjectivity. It is these disciplines which aim to explore that which is creative and humanistic. Subjectivity is essential for the writer who would create a fascinating character in a novel. It is necessary to build a figure who has an interesting view of the world.

Thus some areas or disciplines are primarily associated with either objective or subjective knowledge. Social studies education, however, tends to range across both perspectives. It is likely that curriculum will be based at least in part on what the social sciences offer as objective knowledge about man and society. It is also likely that the curriculum will reflect subjectivity. Personal values, unique descriptions, private language and interpretations will be part of what is considered social studies curriculum. It is conceivable that within the same social studies course during a year students might engage in research using the methodology of social science and also hold a sensitivity session. The first is essentially objective while the second is essentially subjective. Both can lead to knowledge about man and his society.

It would be a herculean task to systematically examine the total range of objective and subjective knowledge that has bearing on the social studies curriculum. We do, however, in the following chapters, offer a basic analysis of the three logical components described above. We see these as the fundamental building blocks which promise to contribute to a more systematic and consistent rationale for social studies curriculum. Chapter 2 offers an analysis of concepts which clarifies how they contribute to the development of categories of knowledge. Criteria for the meaning of the term *concept* are suggested as a way to eliminate some of the ambiguity that has grown around the use of the term. Chapter 3 distinguishes between concepts used to develop descriptive statements and those used to develop valuative statements. Chapter 3 also expands our analysis of the objective-subjective views of knowledge and how they contribute to corresponding curriculum perspectives. Chapter 4 deals with the nature of generalizations that arise out of history and social science research. The problem of developing objective generalizations of the type found in the natural sciences is discussed at some length. Chapter 5 describes the nature of scientific explanation and how it relates to objective explanations in social studies. Chapter 6 is concerned with an alternative view of explanation that is more subjective than the science model. Here we explore a kind of compromise model of explaining human behavior that possesses a wide range of usefulness and interest to those in social studies. The last chapter offers some of the conclusions and implications of our analysis.

The Nature of
Concepts

2

Introduction

In the past several years the term *concept* has received considerable attention in the development of social studies curricula, yet much semantic confusion still surrounds the meaning of the term. One social studies teacher has written that in most cases the word is used with an almost systematic ambiguity and is rapidly reaching the point at which it will become useless for effective discourse.[1]

The purpose of this chapter is to shed some light on the ambiguity surrounding *concept* by presenting an analysis of various meanings which have been given to it. In addition, the writers shall offer a meaning that they believe to be most fruitful for developing and teaching social studies curricula. (The reader should note carefully the headings and progres-

[1] Richard F. Newton, "Concepts, Concepts, Concepts," *Social Education* (January, 1968), p. 2.

sion of ideas within this chapter. An understanding of this material is necessary for precise comprehension of distinctions made in subsequent chapters.)

Concepts as Ideas or Abstractions

Most people think of concepts as ideas or abstractions. The following statements illustrate ways in which professional educators as well as laymen commonly use the term concept as a synonym for idea.

> What is your idea of justice?
> What is your concept of justice?
>
> What idea accounts for how societies change?
> What concept accounts for how societies change?
>
> What is your idea of a good social security system?
> What is your concept of a good social security system?
>
> What is the idea around which the marketing system operates?
> What is the concept around which the marketing system operates?

For many an idea is a concept and a concept is an idea.

Educational psychologists, philosophers, and educators often define a concept as an abstraction. In so doing, they think of a concept as consisting of characteristics or properties common to a set of objects which in their concrete form are different in many respects. Osgood, for example, views concept formation as acquisition of a mediating process that can be detached or abstracted from the stimulus objects with which it may have been associated.[2] Carroll defines a concept as an abstraction from a series of experiences which define a class of objects or events.[3] Jerome Bruner views concept formation as a process of categorizing. Regarding this process he states:

> To categorize is to render discriminably different things equivalent, to group the objects and events around us into classes, and to respond to them in terms of their class membership rather than their uniqueness.[4]

Thus for Bruner a concept is a category. Each of the above definitions suggests that to conceptualize is to abstract and that to possess a concept is to possess an abstraction.

[2] Charles E. Osgood, *Method and Theory in Experimental Psychology* (New York: Oxford University Press, 1953), p. 688.
[3] John B. Carroll, "Words, Meanings and Concepts," *Harvard Education Review,* 34 (Spring, 1964), 178.
[4] Jerome Bruner, Jacqueline Goodnow, and George Austin, *A Study of Thinking* (New York: John Wiley and Sons, Inc., 1965), p. 1.

In clarifying the meaning for the term concept, it is not enough just to say that a concept is an idea or an abstraction.[5] One must be more specific and answer several basic questions. First, how narrow or broad can an idea be and still merit the name concept? Another way of asking the same question is, how simple or how complex can an abstraction be and still be designated a concept? Which of the following, for example, denote abstractions that are to be called concepts: terms, statements, explanations, theories? Second, are concepts definitional or factual in nature? That is, do they, by representing classes and categories, only label reality, or do they in addition express factual claims regarding it? Third, are concepts personal abstractions or can they be shared? Is it legitimate to say that your concept of something is different from mine because concepts by definition are personal constructions? This chapter provides an analysis of alternative answers which can be and have been given to these questions.

At this point a word must be said about words. Meanings are not inherently attached to words: they are assigned to them. It makes little sense, then, to say of a stipulated definition of concept, is it true or false? Instead, one must ask, is it clear and is it fruitful? Thus as one reads this chapter, he must judge for himself which meaning for the term concept seems to be the most helpful to him as he builds or teaches social studies curriculum.

Two Basic Definitions Given to the Term Concept

There are two basic definitions that have been given for the term concept. These definitions are basic in the sense that they are general and that they represent alternative views. They are as follows:

1. A concept is a mentalistic container comprised of those characteristics which are thought to be properties common and jointly peculiar to the denotation of a particular set of objects, events, or the like.
2. A concept is a mentalistic container comprised of all the associations one has with a term.

These definitions differ in that the first stipulates that characteristics, in order to be a part of a concept, must meet the criteria of being common and jointly peculiar to a set of examples designated by it. The second definition is more permissive in that all the associations one has with a term can be part of a concept. The differences between these two basic definitions will become clear in the course of this chapter.

[5] For purposes of discussion we shall equate *idea* and *abstraction* and proceed to use the terms interchangeably.

Concepts as Generalizing Abstractions

The first definition stipulates that a concept is a generalizing abstraction. To give substance to the notion of a generalizing abstraction, the definition employs the metaphor of a mentalistic container. As an abstraction, the container within this definition is comprised of characteristics or properties which have been extracted from objects, events or the like and which can be thought of as applying to them. [6] For example, the mentalistic container designated by the term *chair* can be thought of as consisting of such extracted characteristics as "having a back," "having a seat," "having four legs," and "used by one person." As a *generalizing abstraction,* the mentalistic container is comprised of properties common to a number of objects or events. For instance, the mentalistic container denoted by the term chair consists of characteristics which are applicable or can be generalized to more than one instance of chair.

The following illustration may help to clarify the notion of a concept as expressed in the first basic definition:

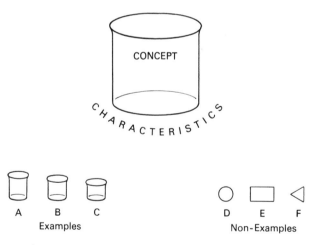

The concept in this illustration may be thought of as constructed of characteristics which denote or point to various examples. It permits certain objects (A, B, C) to pass into it while it does not permit others (D, E, F). Another way of expressing it is to say that the container is constructed so that objects A, B, and C logically fit into it. Objects D, E,

---

[6] There are several views concerning the nature of extraction as it is involved in the process of abstraction. For our purposes, we shall think of extraction as focusing on, attending to, or identifying certain properties of objects at the exclusion of others.

and F will not because they do not exhibit the necessary characteristics. That the container consists of extracted characteristics makes it an abstraction. That it relates to more than one object permits it to be thought of as a generalizing abstraction.

Consistent with this first definition, a concept can also be thought of as a pair of glasses through which one views the world. The glasses consist of certain characteristics or properties which permit one to see some objects as examples and others as nonexamples.

BREADTH AND COMPLEXITY OF CONCEPTS AS GENERALIZING ABSTRACTIONS

There have been several kinds of generalizing abstractions that have been called concepts. In order to explicate these subforms, it is helpful to return to the three questions posed above. First, what is the breadth or complexity of abstractions thought of as concepts from this point of view? Several answers have been given to this question and each helps to establish a more specific meaning for the term concept.

First, there are those who limit a concept to abstractions designated by *terms*.[7] According to this point of view, "whale," "person whose salary is less than three thousand dollars a year," "friendly," and "made of cloth" are concepts. Note that concepts so conceived can be designated by nouns, nouns with their modifiers and adjectives, or adjectives with their modifiers. Note that such concepts do not assert that something is the case, i.e., they do not make factual claims. They simply categorize phenomena.

To form a concept from this way of thinking is to establish the criteria for the use or meaning of a term. To teach a concept is to teach the criteria to someone. Constructing and teaching concepts from this point of view are definitional ventures.

In accordance with the notion that a concept is a term, the word *artifacts,* meaning "simple objects showing human workmanship or modification," designates a concept which represents a container permitting pencils, paintings, and houses to fit into it as examples, and trees and wildlife to be screened out as nonexamples. The task of the person constructing or teaching a concept such as artifact is to clarify the criteria for the meaning of the term by entertaining various characteristics and examples that can get the job done.

It is important to note that concepts thought of as generalizing abstrac-

---

[7] Although precise writing requires one to say that a term designates or denotes a concept, we shall be less strict in our writing and equate a concept and a term. Thus we are not making a distinction between the symbol and the referent even though such distinction can be made.

tions are designated only by general terms. Concerning this point, May Broadbeck writes:

> Some of the words in a sentence refer to individual things, either simple or complex, like John or Minnesota. Others refer to characters or attributes of individual things or relations among them. All such words are called descriptive terms. Those which name not individual things, but their character and relations are concepts of science.[8]

According to Broadbeck, concepts are classifications applicable to more than one individual thing.

Several of the federally funded social studies projects which draw heavily from the social sciences for their content define a concept as an abstraction denoted by a general term. One example is Project Social Studies at the University of Minnesota which defines conceptualizing as the process of categorizing and a concept as a classification.[9] Among the general terms which they offer as examples of concepts are mountains, voting, manufacturing, socialization, marriage, conservative, and temperature.[10] In addition to the Minnesota project the social studies curriculum program at Syracuse University has developed an interdisciplinary list of thirty-four concepts (general terms) that serve as a basis for constructing curriculum.[11] Yet another example of this approach to curriculum development is found within the revised version of the Wisconsin Conceptual Framework.[12]

So far, much has been said about a point of view that stipulates that a concept is an abstraction designated by a general term. There are, however, some who accept the general formulation but indicate that one does not necessarily need a name for a concept in order to say that he has formed or possesses it. One formulation asserts that concepts can exist without verbal symbols. Travers states, "Attaching a word to a concept so that it is conventionally labeled is not an essential part of the concept-attainment process." [13] John Wilson argues in the same vein when he writes, "It is quite possible to have a concept of something, but for there to exist no single word—not even a word invented by the per-

---

[8] May Broadbeck, "Logic and Scientific Method in Research on Teaching," in N. L. Gage, ed., *Handbook of Research on Teaching* (Chicago: Rand McNally and Co., 1963), p. 45.

[9] Edith West, "Concepts, Generalizations, and Theories," Background Paper No. 3, University of Minnesota, p. 1.

[10] Ibid., p. 1.

[11] Roy Price, Warren Hickman, and Gerald Smith, *Major Concepts for the Social Studies* (Syracuse, N.Y.: Syracuse University Press, 1965).

[12] Wisconsin Department of Public Instruction, "A Conceptual Framework for the Social Studies," Bulletin No. 145, rev. ed., 1967.

[13] Robert M. W. Travers, *Essentials of Learning* (New York: The Macmillan Company, 1967), p. 143.

son who has the concept—which describes the thing." [14] In regard to this, one might cite a conceptual response as an indication of the presence of a concept, yet have no name for the concept which produced it.

On the other hand, two positions have been offered to characterize the point of view that abstractions must include names if they are to be called concepts. Hunt, Marin, and Stone, defining a concept as "a decision rule, which when applied to the description of an object, specifies whether or not a name can be applied" [15] seem to say that to have a concept is also to have a name. Henderson more directly indicates this position when he observes that it is verbal rather than nonverbal concepts which are part of the subject matter of the school. His definition of a verbal concept requires some kind of relation between a term and its use.[16] The position that concepts necessarily involve terms seems to have merit as one reflects on the task of building a social studies curriculum.

The position that a concept is a term is a relatively simple and narrow stipulation as compared to the more complex and broad position that a concept is a statement or an explanation or a theory. It is more simple or narrow in that combinations of terms help to comprise statements, explanations, and theories. Likewise, statements, explanations, and theories are more broad and complex constructions.

While some stipulate that concepts are terms, others contend that concepts are statements. To comprehend this view of a concept, one must understand the nature of a statement. A statement is an expression which asserts that something is the case. It makes a truth claim. Linguistically it is an independent clause rather than a word or phrase. As such it relates at least two or more terms. For example, the statement "President Nixon has wavy hair," relates the term "wavy hair" to the term "President Nixon." [17] The statement "all objects fall at the rate of thirty-two feet per second per second" relates the term "falling at the rate of thirty-two feet per second per second" to the term "objects." The first statement is singular in that the characterisic "wavy hair" is applied to *one* object, "President Nixon." The latter statement is general in that it relates the characteristic "falling at the rate of thirty-two feet per second per second" to *any number* of dropped objects. Although it is conceiv-

---

14 John Wilson, *Thinking with Concepts* (Cambridge, Mass.: University Printing House, 1966), p. 56.

15 Earl B. Hunt, Janet Marin, and Philip Stone, *Experiments in Induction* (New York: Academic Press, Inc., 1966), p. 10.

16 Kenneth B. Henderson, "Teaching Mathematical Concepts" (unpublished manuscript, 1968), p. 33.

17 Note that according to the first basic definition, the term "President Nixon" is not a concept because it represents an *individual* unit. Thus for those who accept the first subposition, all concepts are terms, but not all terms are concepts.

able that one may wish to call singular statements concepts, it has been primarily general statements that have been called concepts.

In discussions with professional educators, the writers have heard the following kinds of general statements offered as concepts:

1. If a superordinate goal is added to a situation in which there is inter-group conflict, the conflict will be reduced.
2. If a division of labor is employed there will be an increased productivity and a rising standard of living.
3. Man's development of human traits and his perceptions of himself as a particular personality derive from his group associations.

Although most recent social studies projects have not called general statements concepts, common usage suggests that many teachers think of them as such.

Concepts thought of as general statements categorize *truth claims.* The following illustration may help to clarify this point:

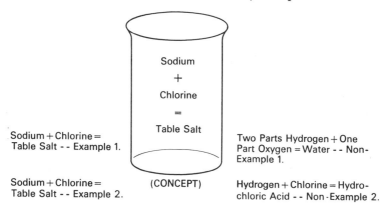

Sodium + Chlorine = Table Salt - - Example 1.

Sodium
+
Chlorine
=
Table Salt

Two Parts Hydrogen + One Part Oxygen = Water - - Non-Example 1.

Sodium + Chlorine = Table Salt - - Example 2.

(CONCEPT)

Hydrogen + Chlorine = Hydro-chloric Acid - - Non-Example 2.

The truth claim which is categorized in this illustration is that if sodium and chlorine are added in equal parts, one obtains table salt. As a generalizing abstraction the concept points to or denotes a number of examples in the real world. Example 1 represents one instance in which equal parts of sodium and chlorine are combined to yield table salt. Example 2 represents another instance of the same phenomenon. Both of these examples fit logically into the mentalistic container. Nonexamples 1 and 2 represent combinations of elements which do not logically fit into the container.

To form a concept, conceived as a general statement, is to form a general truth (generalization). To teach a concept from this point of view is to teach a general truth to someone.

While some educators have called terms concepts and others have called statements concepts, a number of others have called explanations and theories concepts. A complete explication of explanations and theories as concepts cannot be given at this point because it is difficult to adequately indicate the nature of each within the limits of this chapter. Both constructions, however, will be given attention later in the book.

More simply, explanations and theories can be thought of as generalizing abstractions which point to examples in the real world. Both help to clarify why objects and events occur the way they do. Both help to answer "why" questions. For example, it is not uncommon to hear a teacher say that he is going to teach the concept of Turner's thesis or the Malthusian theory. To teach these concepts would be to show someone how these constructions clarify why certain social phenomena occur the way they do.

To summarize the basic view that a concept is a generalizing abstraction, there are three subdefinitions: (1) concepts are general terms (2) concepts are general statements (3) concepts are explanations or theories. In response to the first of the three clarifying questions posed earlier in this chapter, what do these views suggest about the breadth or complexity of concepts thought of as generalizing abstractions? These views suggest that there is variation within this general position. Subdefinition 1 is relatively narrow and simple in construction. Subdefinition 2 is broader and more complex. Subdefinition 3 is even more so.

DEFINITIONAL OR FACTUAL NATURE OF CONCEPTS AS
GENERALIZING ABSTRACTIONS

The second clarifying question which needs to be asked of the basic position that concepts are generalizing abstractions is whether concepts are definitional or factual in nature. In other words do they, by representing classes and categories, only definitionally group elements of reality, or do they, in addition, express factual claims about them? There are several answers to this question.

The position that concepts are terms necessarily holds that concepts are definitional in nature. Although terms become involved in factual assertions, as terms they represent meanings which have been based on some particular definition. It can be said of a concept thought of as a term that it can be defined, but it cannot be proved true or false.

The view that concepts are statements suggests a different answer to the above question. As was discussed earlier, statements, by definition, make a truth claim. Thus, one would likely conclude that concepts conceived as statements are factual in nature. This is valid, but only to the degree that it represents one of two ways of looking at truth.

There are two kinds of truth. The view of truth with which one is most likely familiar is that the truth or falsity of a statement is contingent on evidence from the real world. This kind of factual truth has been called *synthetic truth*. The general statements listed earlier in the chapter are examples of synthetic truths which some social studies teachers have called concepts. There is, however, another view of truth which asserts that some statements may depend upon their *form* for their truth. Such statements have been called *necessary* or *analytic truths*. They require no evidence from the real world to support them as true. Definitional statements represent one kind of analytic statement.

For a clarification of the meaning of an analytic statement consider the following example. "All formal rules help groups to solve common problems." If one defines a formal rule as a rule employed to help solve group problems, the truth of this claim is not dependent upon evidence from the real world but upon the stipulation of how language is to be used. Definitionally, a rule is just not a formal rule unless it is employed to solve group problems. The truth or falsity of this general statement is found within the form of the statement, e.g., by stipulation, the term formal rule is equated with the definition "rule employed to solve group problems." The definition is a necessary truth.

The point is that there are two possible kinds of general statements: synthetic (factual) and analytic (definitional). Both kinds of general statements have been called concepts.

In some cases curriculum developers include both kinds of general statements in their programs and call them concepts. This seems to be the case in the trial version of the High School Geography Project. Within their conceptual overview of unit 9, *Geography in an Urban Age,* they provide several statements which they label as "Basic Concepts." The following is an excerpt from this overview:

> A. Basic Concept: Any politically organized group operates within a well-defined area known as its political territory. Within this political territory there is a political hierarchy which has a territorial framework.
>
> > 1. All governments and other political groups operate within a well-defined area known as their political territory.
> > 2. Within any political territory there is a political hierarchy which has both a horizontal and a vertical division of functions and power. . . .
>
> B. Basic Concept: Within and among political units, there is a spatial structure to political organization and political processes.
>
> > 1. Physical, cultural, and economic differences from place to place give

rise to associated differences in political ideals and goals. These differences are reflected in political behavior of people and their representatives.

2. The location of seats of government, public functions (e.g., military bases, airports, schools, and hospitals), and the awards of government contracts generates conflict. . . .[18]

It is difficult to tell if each general statement in sections *A* and *B* is a basic concept, or if together each entire section constitutes a basic concept, or whether only the first statement in each section is a basic concept. It is also somewhat difficult to tell within the limited context if the statements are factual or definitional. There does, however, appear to be a mixture of factual and definitional general statements which individually or together are thought of as basic concepts.

Statements in section A, for example, appear to focus on a definition of the term *political territory*. Thus, as concepts, these general statements seem to be definitional. Statements in section B vary. The first statement can possibly be interpreted as a definition of a political unit and thus can be thought of as a definitional concept. The subpoints under B, however, appear to make assertions, the truth of which is dependent on evidence from the social world. These substatements, as concepts, appear to be factual.

Again, the point is that some have called general factual statements concepts. Others have called general definitional statements concepts. Still others have called both kinds concepts. Whereas concepts thought of as general terms are necessarily definitional in nature, concepts thought of as general statements can and have been thought of as factual and/or definitional in nature.

The position that concepts are explanations or theories also has definitional and factual forms. Scientific explanations and theories are factually based. Mathematical explanations derive from axioms and basic definitions. Thus, concepts viewed as explanations and theories can and have been thought of as factual or definitional constructions. In social studies, however, explanations and theories are factual in nature.

Thus in response to the second clarifying question concerning the definitional or factual nature of concepts conceived as generalizing abstractions, it can be said that (1) concepts as general terms necessarily represent definitional claims (2) concepts as general statements have been thought of as factual or definitional claims (3) concepts as explanations and theories have also been thought of as factual or definitional assertions.

[18] Roger E. Kasperson, Trial Version Guidelines for Unit 9: *Political Process,* The High School Geography Project's Geography in an Urban Age (Boulder, Colo.: Association of American Geographers, 1966), pp. xi-xii.

OBJECTIVE OR SUBJECTIVE NATURE OF CONCEPTS AS GENERALIZING ABSTRACTIONS

The third question which needs to be answered in order to understand the nature of concepts thought of as generalizing abstractions is whether concepts, so conceived, are personal or shared constructions. In other words, are concepts, thought of as generalizing abstractions, subjective or objective in nature?

Looking at concepts as generalizing abstractions, one might hold a concept subjectively or objectively. A generalizing abstraction designated by a term might be one that is unique to an individual or one that is commonly shared. Meanings of social science concepts (terms) must be shared since social science is an objectively-based enterprise. Other concepts (terms) might represent unique abstractions. Such unique concepts might be held by a pioneer on the frontier of knowledge as he creates new categories or by a small child as he makes sense of the world from his own limited experience. Such concepts also might be held by one as he conjures up characteristics that he believes to be associated with a particular category. Communism, for example, has different meanings for different people.

Concepts as statements also may be held subjectively or objectively. Thus any general statement may be held uniquely by one individual or it can be held in common with others. For the latter case to exist, terms within the statement must have commonly shared meanings, and the expressed relationship between or among them must be understood.

The following two concepts (general statements) can be subjectively or objectively held:

1. In fascist countries, people are servants of the state rather than served by the state (general analytic statement).
2. Democracy has survived because of the role played by political parties (general synthetic statement).

The first general statement is objective to the degree that there is agreement about the meaning of the terms in the statement and agreement that the term fascist country should be defined as one in which a person serves the state rather than being served by it. The degree to which there is lack of agreement on these matters, the statement is subjective. Likewise, the second general statement is objective to the degree that there are common meanings for the terms found in it and that there is also a common understanding of the meaning of the dependence relationship which is implied. (The statement implies that "survival of democracy" has been *dependent on* the role played by political parties.)

Like general statements (and for the same reasons), explanations and theories can also be held subjectively and objectively.

Subjectivity and objectivity, as they apply to concepts, general statements, explanations, and theories, will be a central theme throughout this book. It is sufficient in this chapter to note that concepts thought of as generalizing abstractions can be subjectively or objectively held.

SUMMARY OF CONCEPTS THOUGHT OF AS
GENERALIZING ABSTRACTIONS

In summarizing the basic position that concepts are generalizing abstractions, it can be said that there are three subpositions: (1) concepts are general terms (2) concepts are general statements (3) concepts are explanations or theories. Concepts thought of as general terms are relatively simple abstractions, definitional in nature, and subjectively or objectively held. Concepts thought of as general statements are somewhat more complex abstractions, definitional or factual in nature, and subjectively or objectively held. Concepts thought of as explanations or theories are relatively complex abstractions, definitional or factual in nature, and subjectively or objectively held. As was stated earlier, explanations and theories in the social studies are primarily factual in construction.

*Concepts as all the Associations
One Has with a Term*

The second of the two basic definitions of the term concept stipulates that a concept is a mentalistic container comprised of all of the associations one has with a term. Hullfish and Smith help to clarify this definition of a concept as they discuss the nature of what they call a "conceptual response." [19] Believing that attempts to account for human behavior by focusing on generalizing abstractions about such behavior have been fruitless, they prefer not to give attention to concepts thought of as generalizing abstractions. In fact, they do not wish to use the term concept at all.[20] Instead, they choose to focus on the mindful and purposeful responses of individuals as these responses become a part of their unique and distinctive histories. Concepts thought of as generalizing abstractions are seen by Hullfish and Smith as too static and barren to account for the richness of human actions. Thus why incorporate the notion of a concept in one's thinking at all?

[19] H. Gordon Hullfish and Philip G. Smith, *Reflective Thinking* (New York: Dodd, Mead and Co., 1967), chap. 10.
[20] Ibid., p. 149.

Although Hullfish and Smith do not want to use the term concept in accounting for human behavior, their analysis suggests that if they did wish to do so, it would mean "all of the associations one has with a term." This will become more clear with the presentation of their thinking about the nature of the conceptual response.

A conceptual response, according to Hullfish and Smith, exists whenever an individual responds to an *object as suggested* rather than to a *thing as directly presented*.[21] They say, for example, that a person will respond to an actual dog in terms of the "conglomeration of qualities suggested to him by the term dog."[22] A dog may be "a thing to play with," "a thing at which to throw rocks," "a thing that barks and bites," etc. The term dog will bring a suggested object into the experience of a person that is as rich or poor in meanings as his past experiences with dogs have been varied or limited.[23] A suggested object, as it consists of the sum of the qualities associated with a term could be called a concept. From this perspective, a concept permits a person to interpret a situation, and it thus provides him with a resource for making a conceptual response.

A concept in this sense consists of all the associations one has with a term. Rather than consisting of a set of definitional characteristics, a concept, according to this second basic definition, consists of all the connotative or contingent characteristics associated with a term. Connotative or contingent characteristics are those characteristics which experience has shown to be associated with defined objects or events. Hullfish and Smith see these associations, rather than generalizing abstractions, as a significant foundation on which conceptual behavior rests.

The following example may help to indicate the difference between definitional and contingent characteristics that may be associated with a term. Definitional characteristics associated with the term radio are: "a receiving set," and "permits wireless reception of electrical impulses by means of electric waves." Possible contingent characteristics associated with the term are: "permits one to find out what is going on in the world," "used to provide entertainment when one is bored," "can play music by which to put the baby to sleep," "if dropped, may likely break," "if left on for a long time will become inoperative," "may have a plastic case," and "something to prize."

A concept thought of as all the associations one has with a term consists of a conglomeration of qualities. A concept, thus defined, does not require that all qualities are consistent and harmonious. For example,

21 Ibid., p. 157.
22 Ibid., p. 158.
23 Ibid., p. 157.

the concept, radio, may be thought of as "something which should be used to play background music for a candlelight dinner," *and* "something which should *not* be used to play background music for a candlelight dinner."

Concerning the conglomeration of associations, Hullfish and Smith write:

> Moreover though one may respond appropriately . . . by virtue of the potentialities of this conglomeration of qualities, the response can hardly be itself conglomerate, moving in all directions at once; nor will it be conceptual if it moves serially through the gamut of potential meanings possessed. The function of the conceptual response is the discovery of a plan for responding to . . . [an actual object] by first responding, at the level of meanings, to . . . [an object as suggested].[24]

Concepts, stipulated as all the associations one has with a term, are broad conglomerations of meanings which in their interrelationships suggest further meanings. They permit one to make an interpretation of a unique object or event and serve as a source upon which one can draw to creatively and intelligently bring about a response. It should also be said that additional experience may help add to the breadth of the construction.

Thus, in response to the three questions raised earlier, it can be said that (1) The second basic definition represents a broad, complex construction designated only by a term. (2) Although concepts according to this point of view are comprised of associations of experiences with actual objects in the real world, as associations they function, loosely speaking, to define (interpret) a situation, rather than to make a contingent claim about a situation. Concepts thus conceived are constructions which permit one to say, "Here is a situation in which if I respond in *x* manner, *y* consequences will result." (3) Concepts thought of as all the associations one has with a term are personal constructions. Just as no two people have the same experiences with objects in their environment, no two people will have the same concepts of these objects. Therefore this basic definition stipulates that a concept is a *subjective* rather than an objective construction.

While the writers know of no particular social studies program that is based on this second basic definition of a concept, common usage suggests that many social studies teachers assume this position in their use of the term.

---

24 Ibid., p. 159.

*Rationale for the Two Basic
Definitions of the Term Concept*

Each of the two basic definitions of the term concept rests on a different rationale. The following appears to be the thinking of those in social studies who call generalizing abstractions concepts:

1. There are regularities in the social world, i.e., social behavior can be categorized.
2. Man, in attempting to reach his social goals, may intelligently do so by taking into account these regularities.
3. Social regularities are comprehended and expressed in the form of generalizing abstractions.
4. The term concept can be used to denote instances of generalizing abstractions.

Those who think of concepts as all the associations one has with a term seem to do so from the following rationale:

1. Man, because he has the ability to establish a wide variety of purposes, does not always act in regular ways.
2. A person can best interpret and respond to unique situations by drawing on his background of conglomerate knowledge.
3. Since objects and events are given names, such knowledge is effectively organized in the form of sets of factual associations one has with a term.
4. The term concept can be used to denote instances of these sets of factual associations.

The position of concepts as generalizing abstractions suggests a focus on that which is similar. The view that concepts are all the associations one has with a term implies an emphasis on the personally unique. The first position directs one to focus on limitation and logical implication. The second position suggests attention to scope and psychological implication. While the first directs attention away from a perceiver, the latter construction implies an emphasis on the perceiver and his psychological construction. The first position seems consistent with attempts to make scientific explanations of human responses. The latter seems quite consistent with the rational reconstruction approach of accounting for human behavior.[25] In short, thinking of a concept as a generalizing

---

[25] The rational reconstruction approach emphasizes accounting for social behavior by "getting under the skin" of a historical agent and then attempting to think and feel the way the agent felt prior to some event, i.e., to put on the agent's conceptual glasses to psychologically account for social actions or events.

abstraction is primarily to be logically set; while thinking of a concept as all the associations one has with a term is primarily to be psychologically oriented.

Selection of a Meaning for the Term Concept

Which of the two basic definitions of a concept is the most fruitful for purposes of developing social studies curriculum? In some ways the second definition seems more valid as one thinks about the way in which he goes about responding to everyday situations. Ordinarily, we encounter some social phenomenon for which we have a name; we recall possible meanings the phenomenon may have; we look for signals it is producing; we then decide upon a particular response to it. For example, a frown on a professor's face in response to a student's contribution in class is judged and acted on by a student drawing on all the associations he has with the frowning, judging the signals given in the particular context, and then making a response to it. Several alternative responses which a student can make to the professor's frown are the following: He might say, "You don't like me do you!" "What was wrong with my answer?" "I am sorry for speaking before I thought through the question." The response the student makes will be based on his interpretation of the situation.

The limitation on this notion of a concept is that it focuses primarily on a subjective view of reality. Although the idea that concepts are associations with a term is applicable when one is dealing with personal and unique perceptions, many social issues require common or objective perceptions. For instance, in making legislative decisions which affect significant numbers of people, it is essential that lawmakers share knowledge about possible consequences of alternative courses of actions. In fact, to the degree that any behavior has a significant effect on others, there will be a need to focus on objective perceptions and purposes. In addition, there will be a need to focus on regularities suggested by the definitions of general terms and also on regularities denoted by general contingent statements since social decisions cannot be made for each social object or event encountered in its uniqueness. Thus the position that concepts are generalizing abstractions seems more helpful as one

---

On the other hand, the scientific approach attempts to explain social behavior by subsuming an event or behavior under a law-like statement or statements. To be very useful, law-like statements must be abstract constructions. Therefore, the position that concepts are associations with a term is consistent with the former approach of accounting for behavior while the position that concepts are generalizing abstractions is consistent with the latter approach.

goes about the business of constructing and teaching a broad range of social studies curriculum.

While the position that concepts are associations with a term requires that one analyze social phenomena from a subjective point of view, the position that concepts are general abstractions designated by terms permits social objects and events to be analyzed from either a subjective or objective point of view. That it includes both possible frames of reference makes it attractive for purposes of looking at the various alternative curricular perspectives that can be included within a social studies program. Based on the notion that a concept is a generalizing abstraction designated by a term, several alternative curricular perspectives will be discussed in the next chapter.

Which specific definition of concept as a generalizing abstraction is most useful to the work of the social studies curriculum writer or teacher? Since within the content of social studies many terms designate categories which do not have readily identifiable examples, there is a real need to clarify their definitional meanings. A dog, for example, is much more readily identifiable as an instance of the concept "dog" than is a particular series of events identifiable as an instance of the concept "acculturation." Thus, in social studies, there is a need to draw attention to definitional constructs.

The writers therefore agree with the present trend of calling only terms concepts. To do so helps to give attention to the definitional aspects of social inquiry. Tested generalized knowledge contains both definitional and empirical aspects and thus it is helpful for purposes of comprehending the process and product of social inquiry to separate the abstraction formation process from the testing aspect. That is, one must understand the analytic operations of hypothesis testing as separate from, but related to, the synthetic operations of the process. The former may have an effect on the latter and vice versa, but they are distinct.

To help one keep in mind both parts of publicly verified knowledge, it is appropriate to use terminology that is helpful in indicating and maintaining this distinction. Therefore, for purposes of engaging in social inquiry, the term concept might fruitfully be defined in the following way:

1. Only abstractions designated by terms should be called concepts.
2. Concepts should be thought of as consisting only of the definitional characteristics associated with a term, not contingent ones as well.
3. Only general, as opposed to singular, terms should designate concepts.
4. One must have a name for a concept before it can be said that he has formed or learned it.

While the term concept may be fruitfully employed to point to the definitional, analytic element of social inquiry, other terms such as synthetic statement, synthetic belief, and synthetic generalization might be employed to direct attention to general factual empirical components of the process.

Summary

There has been considerable confusion surrounding the meaning of the term concept. Two basic definitions have been given for the term. First, a concept is a mentalistic container comprised of properties that are common and jointly peculiar to the denotation of a set of objects, events, or the like. Second, a concept is a mentalistic container comprised of all the associations one has with a term. The first definition stipulates that a concept is a generalizing abstraction. Three kinds of generalized abstractions have been called concepts: those designated by (1) general terms (2) general statements (3) explanations and theories. The second basic definition asserts that concepts consist of all the contingent characteristics one associates with a term.

It was concluded that for purposes of comprehending and communicating the nature of the process and product of social inquiry, it is fruitful to call only general terms concepts. Doing so helps to draw attention to the definitional aspects of social inquiry as separate from but related to the synthetic aspects of the investigative process. Doing so also enables one to analyze the subjective and objective ways in which various people look at the social world.

Descriptive and Valuative Concepts

3

Introduction

In the last chapter a distinction was made between two general definitions for the term, concept:

1. A concept is a mentalistic container comprised of characteristics or properties which are common and jointly peculiar to the denotation of a particular set of objects, events, or the like.
2. A concept is a mentalistic container comprised of all the associations one has with a term.

The conclusion reached was that for purposes of understanding the process and product of social inquiry, the first definition has advantages over the second.

From the point of view of the first definition, there are additional distinctions regarding the nature of concepts which should be understood if one is to build comprehensive and consistent social studies curricula. Among them are a number of contrasting ways of classifying concepts. A list of such classifications includes concepts categorized as either easy or difficult, denotative or attributive, singular or general, and descriptive or valuative.[1] Each of these sets of categories has a potential implication for curriculum construction and should be given attention in any full treatment of the nature of concepts. The decision, however, was made to be less complete in this chapter and to focus only on the last of the above-mentioned contrasts, namely *descriptive* and *valuative* concepts. This more limited focus is relevant to a primary task in this book of explicating the subjective-objective dimensions of social studies curricula.

Use of Descriptive and Valuative Concepts

Descriptive and valuative concepts are employed in statements of fact and value. Descriptive concepts are used in making factual assertions about the "real world." Valuative concepts are employed in making assertions about one's interests and preferences within the real world. In the factual statement, "Mr. Johnson is six feet tall," it is asserted that the height of a particular person is an instance of the descriptive concept "six feet tall." In the valuative statement, "Miss Hill is a very good teacher," the valuative concept "very good teacher" is used to express a preference for Miss Hill as well as to categorize her. In short, descriptive and valuative concepts are employed as building blocks in the construction of factual or valuative statements. They aid in accomplishing the factual or valuative purposes of the communication.

With an understanding that the significance of descriptive and valuative concepts is to be found within the context of the statements in which they appear, let us look more closely at their differences and similarities. To do so, consider the following lists of concepts:

List A	*List B*	*List C*
interviewing	rape	strong
membership group	murder	bad
role	thief	beautiful
Presidents of the United States	Communist	undesirable
material culture trait	love	right

[1] For a discussion of a number of these distinctions, see Henry S. Leonard, *Principles of Right Reason* (New York: Holt, Rinehart and Winston, Inc., 1957); Kenneth B. Henderson, "Teaching Mathematical Concepts" (University of Illinois: unpublished manuscript, 1968); and Harry S. Broudy, B. Othanel Smith, and Joe R. Burnett, *Democracy and Excellence in American Secondary Education* (Chicago: Rand McNally, 1964).

Based on our experience with words, we would more than likely characterize concepts in List C as valuative in nature and those in List A as basically descriptive. Concepts such as "good," "bad," "strong," "weak," "beautiful," "ugly," "desirable," "undesirable," "right," and "wrong" house our preferences and interests. A use of "good," for example, generally expresses our preference *for* something. To say that something is "bad" ordinarily expresses a *negative* feeling toward an object, event, or the like.

Concepts in List A, on the other hand, are more neutral. They are descriptive in that they merely tend to categorize various phenomena in the real world and not express a preference for them. "Membership group," for example, neutrally places in a category those groups to which an individual actually belongs, e.g., a family, school, or other social group. The concept gives no hint of one's preferences or interests for any of the groups. In a way, the concepts in List A tell about the way things are and those in List C tell about the way things should be if our preferences and interests were to be satisfied.

Concepts in List B are more troublesome. In some ways they appear quite descriptive. "Rape," for example, does in fact classify a set of actions. Likewise the concept, "thief," denotes a number of people who have certain characteristics in common. To the degree that concepts in this list appear primarily to categorize phenomena, they seem descriptive. On the other hand because of our particular values, we generally have negative feelings about instances of "rape," "murder," "thief," and "Communist," and positive emotions toward examples of "love." To the degree that we do, List B also appears to be valuative. How then shall we label concepts such as those found in List B? What is the nature of the concepts that belong in this group?

One thing for certain is that because preferences and interests vary from person to person and from group to group, it may not be easy to obtain widespread agreement as to which concepts should be included in List B. If we did wish to compile such a list, however, the words would (1) have to be descriptive in form (i.e., in a form other than that which directly signals a rating or evaluation—more like the form of those concepts in List A), and (2) still have to have the capacity to indirectly express preferences and interests.

Whether or not a concept actually belongs in List B is partially a function of context. For example, someone might argue that socialism should also be included in List B. Its form seems primarily to signal a neutral categorization and yet the concept has the capacity to express a preference. Consider, for example, the expression of negative feelings for a particular piece of social legislation by the exclamation, "Why, that bill is nothing but pure socialism!" The person offering the statement is not merely using the concept "socialism" to describe the legislation. Instead, he is communicating a readiness to be against it. How can one tell if a person is actually employing a concept of the type found in List B in a valuative manner? The answer often lies within the context of its use. In the above case, the exclamatory form of the statement in which the concept appears provides a hint that "socialism" is being employed to express a preference. Also, the larger context in which the discussion about the social legislation occurs might help to reveal the intended use of the concept.

It should be emphasized that the context in which a concept is employed may not always offer any clear indication of the function the concept is to perform, i.e., whether it is being employed neutrally to categorize or whether it is being used primarily to express a preference. In this case, one must inquire from the person making the statement his purposes for using the concept. It is common to find classroom discussions in which a teacher and a student or a student and another student are on different wave lengths because of a failure to clarify the intended functions of the concepts employed in their communication.

In short, concepts found in List B represent a mixture of description and evaluation. Since they do, we might label them "mixed concepts." To think of List B concepts as a mixture of description and evaluation suggests that descriptive and valuative categories are not clear-cut. Several questions arise: Are descriptive concepts free from preferences? Do they express preferences as well as categorize? Do valuative concepts categorize phenomena as well as express preferences?

Hunt and Metcalf suggest that descriptive and valuative categories are not mutually exclusive, and thus, to a degree, descriptive concepts are valuative and valuative concepts are descriptive.[2] That descriptive concepts are to a degree valuative can be understood in light of their use. The very fact that one chooses to describe something by using certain concepts and not others is an implicit act of valuation. This can most adequately be understood by reflecting on the use of concepts by scientists. Often times scientists house strong preferences in concepts which to us might seem quite descriptive. On the cutting edge of knowledge in the sciences, pioneers at times carve out totally new concepts in an attempt to make explanations and predictions of phenomena. Certainly, if a scientist feels that the concepts to which he gives birth are more helpful in developing scientific knowledge than are others, his categories or concepts will not be completely neutral with respect to his preferences. Nor will the constructed concepts be neutral with respect to the preferences of other scientists. They will have their own judgments about

2 Maurice P. Hunt and Lawrence E. Metcalf, *Teaching High School Social Studies,* 2nd ed. (New York: Harper and Row, Publishers, 1968), p. 130.

the fruitfulness of the concepts and will thus have positive or negative feelings about their uses and usefulness. To the degree that scientists see particular concepts as helpful or unhelpful in their work, preferences will be implicit in the ways they use them. Focusing attention on one category of perception rather than another is an implicit act of evaluation and an expression of preference. In this sense concepts thought to be descriptive are not purely so.

In addition, one might employ a particular mixed concept (basically descriptive in form) to consciously or unconsciously express a preference. To say of a teacher that his teaching style is *indirect* may be to express a positive or negative preference. As was stated earlier, context can possibly provide a clue as to whether a concept is being used to express a preference and if the preference is positive or negative. Because of the possibility that preferences can be expressed by mixed concepts, descriptive concepts, in the context of their use, may to a degree be valuative.

Besides suggesting that to a degree all descriptive concepts are valuative, Hunt and Metcalf also suggest that all valuative concepts are, to a degree, descriptive.[3] To illustrate this idea, they use the statement, "Mexicans are good agricultural workers." In this statement, "good agricultural workers" would generally be interpreted as a valuative concept, and thus the statement would likely be thought of as an expression of preference for the workers. If the person making the statement were pushed to explain what he means by "good agricultural workers," he might descriptively reply that the concept characterizes those who possess skill, willingness to work, and reliability. Thus he would be indicating that this valuative concept also has a categorizing function. It is in this sense that Hunt and Metcalf believe that all valuative concepts, to a degree, describe as well as express preferences.

Rather than viewing concepts as purely descriptive or purely valuative, Hunt and Metcalf see them on a continuum which they call the *fact-value continuum*. They offer the following illustration of it:[4]

X	X
(statements with clear and agreed upon meanings. Example: This is a red necktie.)	(statements whose terms do not have clear and common meanings. Example: A flared skirt is more attractive than a sheath skirt.)

Although Hunt and Metcalf deal with statements in their construction of the continuum, their primary focus is on the concepts employed

---

3 Ibid., p. 130.
4 Adapted from ibid., p. 131.

in the statements. For them a concept such as "six feet tall" would be placed to the left on the continuum; "good teacher" would be somewhere between the two extremes, perhaps more toward the right; and "good old teacher" to the extreme right.[5]

Although descriptive and valuative concepts are not mutually exclusive constructions, they seem to provide useful categories to separate assertions of "what is" from expressions of preferences. Thus for purposes of constructing social studies curriculum we feel that it is fruitful to employ these distinctions, but with certain qualifications. The first qualification is that valuative concepts should be thought of as those which include rating or evaluative components such as "good," "right," "desirable," and "ugly." If the concept does not include a rating word it is not a valuative concept. For our purposes, then, concepts in List A and List B above are *not* to be thought of as valuative concepts. They may, in a particular context function as expressions of preference, but they should not be thought of as valuative concepts. For purposes of constructing social studies curriculum, concepts in Lists A and B should be thought of as descriptive concepts. There is no direct signaling of an evaluation by these concepts, and since they do not express a preference, they are descriptive in form.

The presence of a rating word is required in order to have an instance of a valuative concept. The writers believe that if this requirement is met then it is more likely that curricular materials will be clear as to their descriptive or valuative purpose. If one wants students to focus on problems concerning preferences, then the students should be working with valuative concepts. If one wants to expose students to elements of preference in statements which include "mixed concepts," then they should translate the mixed concepts into valuative form. For example, in a valuative statement such as, "That bill is nothing but socialism!" the teacher can help students see the valuative nature of the concept "socialism" by having them translate it to mean "bad economic policy" and then having them handle the statement as a valuative statement. The presence of a rating word is essential because it is likely to lead to a clearer distinction between descriptive and valuative content within a social studies curriculum.

Also, in order for a valuative concept to be labeled as such, it must function as an expression of preference. Thus, concepts such as "good policy," "bad government," and "strong president," are valuative concepts to the degree that an individual consciously employs them to express preferences.

[5] For a further treatment of description and evaluation see John Wilson, *Thinking with Concepts* (Cambridge, Eng.: Cambridge University Press, 1963), pp. 40-41; and J. O. Urmson, "On Grading," in Anthony Flew, ed., *Logic and Language* (Oxford, Eng.: Basic Blackwell, 1953), pp. 159-86.

Whether or not a person actually holds the preference he is consciously expressing and whether he holds it with any consideration of the consequences of holding it are questions unrelated to the definition of a valuative concept as stipulated here.[6] In this respect, valuative concepts house trivial as well as significant preferences. It may be possible to cast doubt on the genuineness of an expressed preference, but this would not affect the appropriateness of classifying the concept housing the preference as valuative. In other words, the term valuative concept refers to actual expressions of preference.

Two characteristics, then, should comprise the notion of a valuative concept: (1) a rating word must be used, and (2) the entire construction must function to express a preference.

One caution must be made regarding the identification of an instance of a valuative concept. Usually to employ a positive rating such as "good," "beautiful," or "desirable," in accordance with a particular set of criteria is also to say, "I like that something and am psychologically attracted to it." In other cases (and these are the ones to watch out for) a positive rating of something may not be the same as expressing an attraction toward the rated object. For example, it is possible to say that, "X is good, but I do not like X." It is possible to say, "That was a great football play," and in the same breath say, "But I really didn't like it."

Separation of preference from the positive rating category, "good play" is understandable in the context of a well-executed play made by members of an opposing team. By inferences from the rules of the game and from characteristics of great plays as determined by experts of strategy who have analyzed the game, one might classify a particular football play as great and at the same time think that the play was not so great in the sense that it did not favor the home team. Again, it should be said that context can help to determine the presence of a valuative concept.

Objectivity and Subjectivity as Related to Descriptive and Valuative Concepts

The above definitions might lead one to conclude that descriptive concepts are objective in nature and that valuative concepts are subjective in nature. This conclusion is not valid, nor is it particularly help-

[6] It should be noted that expression of a preference through the vehicle of a valuative concept may not necessarily mean that the person offering the expression in fact holds that preference as a value. Whether or not he does is in part a matter of definition of what a value is and in part a factual concern. For two interesting discussions of what a value is see Hunt and Metcalf, *Teaching High School Social Studies*, pp. 120-64; and Louis Raths, Merrill Harmin, and Sidney B. Simon, *Values and Teaching* (Columbus, O.: Charles E. Merrill Books, Inc., 1966), pp. 27-38.

ful for purposes of explicating all the curricular choices which logically derive from the above definitions of descriptive and valuative concepts.

Instead of concluding that objectivity is a characteristic only of descriptive concepts and subjectivity is a characteristic only of valuative concepts, it makes more sense to think of objectivity and subjectivity as applicable to both kinds of concepts. It is reasonable to say that one can describe reality objectively (through concepts which have common meanings) or subjectively (through concepts which have unique meanings); also that one can express a preference for a particular kind of reality subjectively (through valuative concepts which consist of personally unique sets of criteria) or objectively (through valuative concepts which consist of criteria held in common with a substantial number of people.)

The term "communism" for example, which denotes a descriptive concept, can have a unique or common meaning. Laymen, on the one hand, are likely to have a number of individual meanings for "communism" which makes their use of it subjective in nature. Scholars, on the other hand, relying on the writings of Karl Marx and others, are likely to have common meanings for the term and thus hold and employ the concept objectively.

A valuative concept can also be employed subjectively or objectively. In the valuative question, "Is capital punishment good or bad?" one is asked to rate capital punishment as a good or bad measure for dealing with serious crimes. A response to the question can be made with a unique (individual) set of rating criteria and thus express a subjective valuative judgment; or, it can be made with a common (group) set of criteria and thus express an objective valuative judgment.

Four Curricular Perspectives

Based on the model that descriptive and valuative concepts can be held subjectively and objectively, there are four possible curricular perspectives: [7]

1. Descriptive-objective
2. Descriptive-subjective
3. Valuative-objective
4. Valuative-subjective.

[7] These curricular perspectives should be understood in terms of the focus that the curriculum permits students to have within the courses offered. Another way of stating it is that curricular perspectives are alternative emphases that a curriculum allows students to have within its offerings. In either case, the attention is on student perspective.

The first perspective designates a curricular concern in which the content to be learned is descriptive and objective in nature. In other words, the content to be learned includes concepts which have common meanings and which are used to talk about what is real. This kind of perspective is exemplified in social studies programs which are built around social science concepts, statements, and methodology. The curriculum entitled, "The Sociological Resources for the Social Studies (SRSS)," serves as a clear example of this curricular mode by having students focus on key descriptive concepts and generalizations basic to the discipline of sociology.[8] Encouraging students to think and behave as sociologists, SRSS writers state that, "The sociologist's task is to find out as precisely and accurately as possible what the social realtiy is [as viewed through the sociological concepts]."[9] Since this task is descriptive and objective, the curriculum built around it may also be characterized as descriptive and objective. Other social studies programs which rely heavily on the social sciences for their content tend also to be descriptive-objective in nature.

While it is relatively easy to find examples of social studies programs which are descriptive and objective, it is much more difficult to find examples of ones that are both descriptive and subjective. The writers know of no single social studies curriculum which is built solely around this frame of reference.

There are, however, parts of social studies programs which are consistent with this second curricular focus. One example is found in the lesson or unit in which students are saturated with experiences and then asked to clarify what they have seen, heard, touched, smelled, etc. In this situation a teacher might have students visit an inner-city area to experience the daily living conditions faced by its residents. The account that follows the experience is subjective to the degree that the concepts included in it have personal meanings, have been personally selected for the description, and have been uniquely woven together in the account. Knowledge about social reality gained from such lessons or units is personal and subjective.

Another example of a descriptive-subjective perspective is seen in lessons in which students, relying on their conceptual frames of reference, descriptively talk about the social world. In such lessons, students are permitted to express *their* views concerning the nature of social events—why they occur, their significance. In the open classroom approach, students are even encouraged to help select the subject matter on which

---

[8] "Sociological Resources for the Social Studies," *Instructor's Guide, Inquiries in Sociology*, rev. ed. (Ann Arbor, Mich.: The American Sociological Association, 1968).

[9] Ibid., p. ix.

they will focus. The subjective emphasis of such sessions leads students to share with each other unique and personal frames of reference and points of view.

The rationale behind these lessons is that (1) a society ought to have room for several points of view about the social world; (2) individuals in the society ought not to be forced to perceive social reality through concepts established by some particular group; and (3) understanding the complexity of social reality is enhanced when individuals are exposed to a wide variety of ways of looking at it.

In short, classes in which students talk about social life can be characterized as having a descriptive-subjective orientation.

In addition to the above two examples of a descriptive-subjective curricular perspective, one can also cite as consistent with this approach the beginning lesson in the Holt Social Studies Course entitled, "The Shaping of Western Society." [10] The objectives of the lesson are:

1. To know that classification of information is a function of a person's frame of reference
2. To know that a person's frame of reference is a product of his entire life experience.[11]

In this lesson students discover that a group of words such as "black bass," "collie dog," and "grouse" can be classified in various ways. Not only can they be put in several biological categories, but they can also be classified according to the number of letters or syllables in the word. From this lesson they are to understand that data in the social studies, as perceived from differing frames of reference, can also be classified in various ways. Thus the students are led to see that there is a descriptive-subjective nature to the content of social studies, and indeed to all other fields of inquiry.

The third curricular perspective, valuative-subjective, is exemplified in the approach of Raths, Harmin, and Simon.[12] Believing that values, by definition and by social right are personal constructions, these men see the role of the teacher as that of helping students clarify their own values. In order to do so, they feel it is necessary for a teacher to ask a student such questions as, "Is this something that you prize?" "Did you consider any alternatives to it?" "Would you choose it again?"

They contrast this "clarifying role" with that of setting an example, persuading and convincing, limiting choices, inspiring, offering rules and regulations, presenting cultural or religious dogma, and making appeals

10 Edwin Fenton, ed., *Teacher's Guide for the Shaping of Western Society* (New York: Holt, Rinehart and Winston, Inc., 1968), p. 18.
11 Ibid., p. 18.
12 Raths, Harmin, and Simon, *Values and Teaching.*

to conscience. The theory of teaching values espoused by Raths, Harmin, and Simon assumes that people ought to create their own value systems and that any approach which attempts to impose values is ineffective. Furthermore, these men argue that an individual's behavior becomes positive, purposeful, enthusiastic, and proud only when he has personally examined the values that lie behind his behavior. This personal examination is necessarily shaped and controlled by the individual himself. He must inquire into his own reasons and standards for behavior, and this inquiry is subjective in that an individual must decide for himself in the final analysis what he values. Since this theory of valuing treats value concepts as personally unique, it leads to a curriculum that is valuative-subjective in orientation.

Another example of a valuative-subjective curricular perspective is found in part of the Harvard "jurisprudential" curriculum.[13] Believing that, "when one is pushed to the heart of human values, he must invariably end up accepting some tenet on faith," the Harvard curriculum proposes that social studies ought to focus on processes that provide for:

1. The analysis of controversy in terms of prescriptive, descriptive, and analytic issues
2. The use of distinct strategies for justification and clarification of one's views on such issues
3. Systematic attention to the discussion process as one deals with controversial issues.[14]

These objectives direct a student's attention to the process of valuing rather than to a common, agreed upon set of values to be learned.

The Harvard social studies project accepts as a high-level, given value, the dignity and worth of the individual. But rather than deducing a specific moral code from this general value, they believe that in the process of justifying a particular kind of social conduct, one might appeal to this ultimate value. They also accept and prescribe the teaching of "political process values," that is, those which are defined by the jurisprudential system, e.g., freedom of expression, the right to evaluate and judge governmental leaders, and the right to judicial due process. To the degree that they emphasize the teaching of these values and encourage acceptance of the value that all men should be treated with dignity, their program is valuative-objective in nature.

The Harvard Social Studies project is an interesting combination of

[13] American Education Publications, Columbus, Ohio, has published this curriculum in a series of public issues pamphlets.
[14] Donald Oliver, Fred M. Newmann, and Mary Jo Bane, *Cases and Controversy*, p. 3. These areas are objective in many respects. For example, there are some agreed upon criteria for determining whether a discussion has achieved clarification of a controversial issue.

both objective and subjective approaches. There is heavy emphasis on the objective in the methodology of clarifying public and persisting issues. Thus a variety of strategies is designed to clarify definitional, factual, and valuative problems surrounding a particular controversy. By getting students to define terms clearly, make statements based on factual data, and offer value judgments that explicitly recognize values, the public issues approach is focusing on the objective—descriptive and valuative.

At the root of this approach, however, is a valuative-subjective position. Students are being asked to bring their own views to a public controversy and then justify those views. Individuals use argument and persuasion, as well as clarification processes, to convince others of a particular position. Personal (subjective) views are presented and defended in the course of a public issue discussion. The goal of the Harvard curriculum in the final analysis is to have students clarify their own views. There is no assumption that students should or will come to a consensus on what policy should be pursued, i.e., which policy is best or right. The curriculum is considered successful if a variety of personal and unique viewpoints have been clarified and made consistent for those who hold them. In addition, it is hoped that the process of clarifying personal viewpoints will contribute to a general understanding and resolution of social controversy.

The fourth curricular perspective, valuative-objective, is included as a major emphasis in the positions developed by Hunt and Metcalf and Michael Scriven.[15] Running through their analyses is the argument that an event, object, or policy can be evaluated by testing the factual consequences flowing from it. For example, if one is trying to decide which dishwasher on the market is the best one, criteria can be established for the best dishwasher—e.g., washes dishes cleanest in the least amount of time—and then various models can be tested to determine which one meets the critera. By establishing clear and agreed upon criteria for the valuative concept under consideration, the valuative problem is reduced to a factual or empirical one.

This approach to arriving at valuative judgments is effective in settling interpersonal differences only to the extent it is possible to arrive at clear and agreed upon criteria for valuative concepts employed in the judgments. There must be consensus on what makes something good or best or right. In a situation where there are interpersonal disagreements over what constitutes the criteria for a valuative judgment, testing of factual consequences can not possibly lead to any common conclusions. Thus if some people were to define the best dishwasher as the one that occupies

---

15 See Hunt and Metcalf, *Teaching High School Social Studies;* and Michael Scriven, "Student Values as Educational Objectives" (publication no. 124 of The Social Science Education Consortium).

the least amount of space, has the lowest noise level, and has the most attractive design, and others were to define it as one that washes dishes cleanest in the least amount of time, there would be no common criteria upon which to judge the factual consequences of the case. The key to arriving at common valuative judgments is frequently found in identifying commonly held valuative concepts which permit a meaningful search for relevant facts.

Disagreements over criteria for valuative concepts occur frequently with sociopolitical problems, and these problems are important in the social studies curriculum. For example, black nationalists and integrationists have different positions based on different valuative criteria. In part, they differ on what constitutes the good society and how it can be achieved. One way of resolving the differences between these two groups is to find common social goals that are expressed in commonly held valuative concepts and then judge which of the competing policies— black nationalism or integration—would more effectively lead to the accepted goals.

For example, it may be found that equality of opportunity is a commonly preferred social end and thus it may be employed as a "fixed" goal toward which the competing policies of black nationalism and integration, if accepted, ought to lead. If it is found empirically that separation of blacks into self-determined communities produces a greater degree of equality of opportunity than does a program of integration, then it should be judged to be the better policy, accepted, and acted upon. If, on the other hand, it is proved factually that integration produces more equality of opportunity than does separation, then it should be judged of more worth. The point is that once general preferences are established, then the facts of the situation can be employed to determine which of the more specific, competing social or political preferences should be accepted, at least by that group.

To the degree that a social studies program is built upon the assumption that it is possible and desirable to find common preferences which can be employed in reflectively testing alternative social policies, it is valuative-objective in nature. Another way of saying it is that to the degree that a social studies program focuses on commonly held valuative concepts in their attempts to solve valuative problems, it has a valuative-objective perspective.

Hunt and Metcalf, by building a social studies curriculum on the assumption that democratic and scientific values are worth fostering and ought to be employed in the resolution of valuative problems, offer a valuative-objective perspective.[16] Likewise Scriven offers a program which is also valuative-objective in its perspective. He believes that value posi-

---

[16] Hunt and Metcalf, *Teaching High School Social Studies.*

tions can be validated by a practical method of value reasoning and are defensible in the same way that eating is defensible, i.e., as means to human ends, and that values provide a basis for social action no more and no less empirical than the basis for engineering actions. Thus Scriven's belief that rationality should be commonly shared and applied to the valuative area leads one to conclude that his social studies proposal also includes a major emphasis on a valuative-objective perspective.[17]

Implications for the Development of Social Studies Curriculum

Several implications for social studies curriculum development arise from the analysis presented in this chapter. First, those who build curriculum need to be conscious of the four major perspectives—descriptive-objective, descriptive-subjective, valuative-objective, valuative-subjective—in order to maintain consistency between the goals espoused for their curriculum and the specific content, activities, and evaluation techniques incorporated into the curriculum. In other words, there must be a consistency between means and ends. If, for example, a teacher has the goal of getting students to clarify their own values, it is essential to provide experiences that are valuative-subjective in nature. Similarly, it would be inconsistent to have students consider questions of value when the curriculum is designed to give a descriptive-objective understanding of accounts of social phenomena.

A second implication is that any social studies curriculum which purports to be comprehensive must give some attention to each of the four perspectives. To accomplish this, teachers must be able to identify each perspective. Although a teacher may wish to emphasize one particular perspective because of the needs and interests of his students and society, students should have experiences with each of them. No one focus would be without some value for students engaged in social inquiry.

A third implication is that students, as well as teachers, need to be able to distinguish among the alternative perspectives if they are to understand the nature of the knowledge with which they are working. They need to know that there are different ways of viewing the world and that these produce different kinds of knowledge. An awareness of the distinctions between subjective and objective description, for example, is necessary for a basic understanding of social science. Furthermore, an awareness of the four perspectives will provide an understanding of the difference between personal and social knowledge.

It is important to see that each of the four perspectives is able to con-

17 Scriven, "Student Values As Educational Objectives," p. 10.

tribute to man's picture of the world. Otherwise students may think that only certain ways of viewing the world can produce legitimate knowledge. A strict emphasis on the descriptive-objective perspective could result in students believing that the valuative-subjective approach does not lead to important insights. It has, of course, been traditional in social studies to rely on descriptive-objective content. Again, from the standpoint of comprehensiveness it is important for students to gain experience in arriving at knowledge from all four perspectives.

Finally, by distinguishing among the four perspectives, it is possible for teachers to develop sequence within curriculum. For example, a teacher might establish a goal of having students gain a comprehensive view of contemporary urban life. To achieve this, he might begin by having each student directly experience urban life by visiting a ghetto. This direct experience could then be communicated by the student in a descriptive-subjective manner. Students might write interpretive essays in which they use their own concepts to describe what they saw in the ghetto. They could also discuss from a valuative-subjective perspective their feelings and judgments about urban life. In each of these phases, the emphasis is on the personal and unique perceptions of the person relating his experiences.

From this point, the students might then move to a descriptive-objective stage. They might arrive at an objective account or agreement about how to describe what they saw. Also, they could go to social scientists to find out what experts have said about urban conditions, since frequently it is the goal of social scientists to offer objective descriptions of social phenomena.

Finally, the curriculum could move to a valuative-objective stage in which common valuative concepts are sought with which to judge alternative social policies for solving urban problems.

Throughout this comprehensive approach there might be constant comparisons between subjective and objective perspectives as they are a part of descriptive and valuative phases of the curriculum. Students might be asked to identify when they are operating from unique and common perspectives as well as when they are being descriptive and valuative.

In general, then, the writers are arguing that it is good for people to be conscious of the way they use language and the perspective from which they are viewing the world.

Summary

We began this chapter by saying that a number of distinctions among concepts can fruitfully be made. The distinction which received attention in this chapter was between descriptive and valuative concepts. It was stated that a descriptive concept neutrally categorizes objects and events while valuative concepts express preferences as well as categorize phenomena. Valuative concepts are expressed through rating terms; descriptive concepts are not. Additionally, it was said that certain concepts may be thought of as mixed concepts in that they are descriptive in form but function as expressions of preference.

Based on the distinctions which were made in this chapter between descriptive and valuative concepts, and relying on the differences between subjectivity and objectivity that were discussed in Chapter 1, the conclusion was made that subjectivity and objectivity apply both to descriptive and valuative concepts. This relationship, in turn, suggested that there are four general curricular perspectives on which social studies curriculum can be based: (1) descriptive-subjective, (2) descriptive-objective, (3) valuative-subjective, and (4) valuative-objective.

Those who build or teach social studies curricula need to be conscious of the four perspectives in order to maintain consistency in their curriculum, to be comprehensive, to help students understand the nature of the knowledge with which they are working, and to develop a significant sequence in their programs.

The Nature of
Generalizations

4

Introduction

In the first chapter a brief survey of recent trends in social studies curricula indicated that generalizations have been the focus of much attention. One approach to curriculum development has been to search the literature of the various social sciences for those generalizations that have gained widespread support from authorities in each discipline. These basic generalizations are then used to construct and organize con- ✓ tent and instructional objectives for the social studies classroom.

An example of this approach is found in the Wisconsin *Conceptual Framework for the Social Studies*. The basis of this framework is a set of concepts that are used to develop generalizations encompassing the various disciplines of history and the social sciences. Thus, the following generalization is offered as a basis for developing a tenth-grade history curriculum: "In the process of building and creating a new nation,

Americans were influenced by inherited values, ideas, and institutions as well as by their environment and their experiences." [1]

A similar use of generalizations is found in the Minnesota Project Social Studies. In this curriculum key concepts also serve as the focus of generalization development. For example, a number of generalizations are built around the concept of decision-making. One of several generalizations offered in a twelfth-grade course is: "Any decision is, in part, a product of the internalized values, the perceptions, and the experiences of the persons making the decision." [2]

Another approach to incorporating generalizations into the curriculum is to see them as outcomes of inquiry-centered learning. Thus the end product or conclusion of an inquiry lesson is a tested generalization. For example, Massialas and Cox state that "the end result of social studies instruction is the formulation of generalizations about human affairs." [3] Similarly, Edwin Fenton wants students to develop the ability to handle a mode of inquiry which culminates in a tested generalization.[4] Hunt and Metcalf state that the goal of inquiry is to help students develop insights that lead to generalization. They contend that, "Unless generalization occurs, insight can have little transfer value. Learning which cannot function in making a person's behavior wiser is futile. Teaching, if it is not to be a waste of effort, must lead to generalization." [5] In short, generalizations are seen both as the product of inquiry and as valuable knowledge for the student in directing his behavior.

Role and Function of Generalizations

Those who stress generalizations as a goal of social studies education see this kind of knowledge as more useful and intellectually powerful than singular factual statements. Generalizations are able to show that particular facts and categories relate to each other, and this produces a more accurate and complex view of the world. In moving beyond simple factual statements to generalizations, one obtains a more efficient kind of knowledge. Generalizations serve to summarize more specific knowledge, and thus they provide insights that can be transferred from

---

[1] *A Conceptual Framework for the Social Studies in Wisconsin Schools* (Madison, Wisc.: Department of Public Instruction, 1964).

[2] Project Social Studies Curriculum Center, University of Minnesota, "Africa South of the Sahara," Resource Unit; Grade Twelve (Minneapolis, 1968), p. 4.

[3] Byron Massialas and C. Benjamin Cox, *Inquiry in Social Studies* (New York: McGraw-Hill Book Company, 1966), p. 97.

[4] Edwin Fenton, *Developing a New Curriculum: A Rationale for the Holt Social Studies Curriculum* (New York: Holt, Rinehart and Winston, Inc., 1967), p. 6.

[5] Maurice P. Hunt and Lawrence E. Metcalf, *Teaching High School Social Studies* (New York: Harper and Row, Publishers, 1968), p. 53.

one context to another. In fact, only through generalization can one develop knowledge in one time and place and apply it in another. This is not to claim, however, that all generalizations provide this transfer value. Later in the chapter this point will be clarified.

Social studies curriculum has shown considerable interest in the role of generalization, partly because social scientists frequently attempt to develop generalizations when they engage in research (if not immediately, at least as part of the overall goal of the discipline). Sociologist George Homans indicates that social scientists are engaged in a process of inquiry that leads to discovery and explanation. "Discovery is the job of stating and testing more or less general relationships between properties of nature." [6] This goal of discovering general propositions is the first step in offering explanations for behavior, whether it be the behavior of the economic market place, people in a small group, or some other social situation.

Homans claims there are many generalizations now well-confirmed in the social sciences. For example, "The rate of intergenerational mobility between classes is about the same in all highly industrialized nations. Family instability (divorce, separation, and abandonment) is greatest in the lower class, next in the upper, and least in the middle." [7] According to him, the purpose of developing these generalizations is to provide explanations for social behavior, and to do this effectively it is necessary to relate various general propositions in some kind of theory. Thus generalizations are seen as a means of building theory which in turn provides explanations of a variety of phenomena.

This view is fairly standard among a great number of social scientists.[8] There is wide acceptance among social scientists that they are driving toward the development of propositions on three levels which assert some kind of factual claim that can be tested for its truth or falsity. First, there are singular propositions that assert that a particular phenomenon was observed in a particular place at a particular time. (John F. Kennedy was assassinated in Dallas, Texas, November 22, 1963.) Singular propositions may be accurate, reliable statements, but as such they are not the end product of social science. Second, there are general propositions, or generalizations, that relate types of events. These include

[6] George C. Homans, *The Nature of Social Science* (New York: Harcourt Brace Jovanovich, Inc., 1967), p. 7.

[7] Ibid., p. 19.

[8] For a listing of the various generalizations growing out of the social sciences, see Bernard Berelson and Gary A. Steiner, *Human Behavior: An Inventory of Scientific Findings* (New York: Harcourt Brace Jovanovich, Inc., 1964). For a discussion of social science as theory development, see Hans L. Zetterberg, *On Theory and Verification in Sociology* (New York: The Bedminster Press, 1965), chap. 2.

both statements covering a relatively limited time and space as well as very general propositions using highly abstract concepts and even mathematical symbols. (The Green Bay Packers tend to throw to their tight end on third down and long yardage situations; $e = mc^2$.) Third, there are theories or patterns of related generalizations which are interdependent. (Newtonian mechanics; Adam Smith's classical economics.) Theories range from relatively simple to highly complex formulations. The natural sciences, particularly physics and chemistry, are blessed with a number of reliable theories. Social science appears to have some success in theory construction, for instance in the field of economics, but clearly social science theory is not generally as powerful as that found in many of the natural sciences.

A clear statement of theory building as the goal of political science is offered by David Easton. As he perceives the task of political science, systematic theories of political behavior must be developed. A hallmark of these theories is their ability to explain events of similar types whenever and wherever they occur. He feels that generalizations must be formulated that apply not only to the contemporary scene, but also to history and to other cultures.

Easton goes on to say, "The importance of causal theory lies in the fact that it is an index of the stage of development of any science, social or physical, toward the attainment of reliable knowledge." [9] He suggests that collecting data and making statements about data eventually comes to the point of asking for an explanation of those statements. No one engaged in scientific inquiry is willing to go to considerable effort in accumulating information on a subject unless he believes that information will lead beyond description to generalizing and theorizing about relationships between events. The mere act of collecting certain data and ordering them in the form of singular statements is not sufficient as a goal for science. "The accumulation of data through acceptable techniques does not alone give us adequate knowledge. Knowledge becomes critical and reliable as it increases in generality and internally consistent organization, when, in short, it is cast in the form of systematic generalized statements applicable to large numbers of particular cases." [10]

Clearly the image social scientists like Easton have of their activities comes from a general philosophical position on the nature of scientific inquiry. In recent years there has been a considerable body of philosophical literature addressed to questions concerning the nature and goals of social science inquiry. Social science literature is filled with references indicating a need to clarify philosophical and theoretical questions about

[9] David Easton, *The Political System* (New York: Alfred A. Knopf, Inc., 1953), p. 53.
[10] Ibid., p. 55.

the goals of inquiry in the various disciplines. Unless social scientists are clear as to their overall goals it is not likely they will be able to pursue a consistent and productive line of research.

As indicated in the preceding analysis, all sciences are concerned with developing explanations for phenomena by discovering general relationships or principles that are formulated by determining the conditions under which events occur. The assumption behind this position is that phenomena occur because there are discoverable regularities in nature, i.e., the same conditions consistently result in the same kind of phenomena. To discover these regularities scientists use an objective methodology and language. Thus regularities as expressed by generalizations are the substantive product of objective inquiry into the relationships between events.

R. B. Braithwaite states that the function of the natural and social sciences

> is to establish general laws covering the behavior of the empirical events or objects with which the science in question is concerned, and thereby to enable us to connect together our knowledge of the separately known events, and make reliable predictions of events as yet unknown. The function of establishing general laws is common to all the natural sciences; it is characteristic also of those parts of psychology and of the social sciences which would ordinarily be called scientific as opposed to philosophical. If the science is in a highly developed stage, as in physics, the laws which have been established will form a hierarchy in which many special laws appear as logical consequences of a small number of highly general laws expressed in a very sophisticated manner; if the science is in an early stage of development—what is sometimes called its "natural history" stage—the laws may be merely the generalizations involved in classifying things into various classes.[11]

Once generalizations about a subject are known such knowledge begins to function in further inquiry. The identification of regularities serves to define and anticipate situations. For example, given an economy with stable prices and full employment, a large increase in spending (for example, government spending for a war) will result in rising prices. Such knowledge provides the opportunity to intervene in a situation and take measures to alter the conditions and results. When generalizations serve as guides to action, they are also serving as hypotheses to be tested. By testing and refining the implications of a regularity, further inquiry is taking place and new and more extensive relationships are uncovered. It is the extension and refinement of relationships that produce theories as indicated by Braithwaite.

[11] R. B. Braithwaite, *Scientific Explanation* (New York: Harper and Row, Publishers, 1953), p. 1.

In summary, generalizations serve a number of functions: (1) They serve as conclusions to particular efforts at inquiry. Tested conclusions in the form of generalizations are a legitimate but incomplete conception of the purpose of scientific inquiry. (2) Generalizations also provide the basis for generating new hypotheses, i.e., what else might be true given the implications of a generalization? (3) Generalizations are indispensable in the operations of explanation and prediction. (4) General propositions are basic elements in building scientific theory in that theories consist of interrelated sets of generalizations about generalizations.

Some Characteristics of Generalizations

Thus far generalizations have been treated as if they were all alike, but in fact there are different kinds of generalizations that depend on a number of possible characteristics. It has probably already occurred to the reader that there are a variety of different statements that are commonly called generalizations, and in the preceding section the emphasis was on propositions developed by those engaged in systematic theory building. However, as the historian William Aydelotte has pointed out, there are other purposes for generalizing in some sense of the term, and thus there is a multiplicity of kinds of generalization. It would be a hopeless and arbitrary task to stipulate a single meaning for the term generalization. Nevertheless, it would seem a mistake to say as Aydelotte does that this multiplicity of kinds has created for the term a "vagueness [that] cannot be escaped by elaborating a more precise vocabulary." [12] It is, in fact, both possible and important to provide some precision to our understanding of generalizations in an effort to clarify the implications of having them as an integral part of social studies curricula. In this section a number of distinguishing characteristics of generalizations will be discussed as a way of clarifying differences between kinds of generalizations.

First, in terms of syntactical form, it can be said that all generalizations are statements that assert a relationship between at least two concepts; for instance, "All dogs are four-legged animals." In this statement the general concept "dogs" is related to the concept "four-legged animals." The claim in this statement is that the characteristic of being a four-legged animal is applicable to all instances of the general concept dogs. "Spot is a four-legged animal," is not a generalized statement. This is a singular proposition as opposed to a general one. To put the matter

---

[12] William O. Aydelotte, "Notes on Historical Generalization" in Louis Gottschalk, ed., *Generalization in the Writing of History* (Chicago: University of Chicago Press, 1963), p. 148.

in somewhat technical language, generalizations make a claim about the distribution of a characteristic among the examples denoted by a concept.

Second, in offering a statement that asserts that the examples of a concept have a certain characteristic, a quantification claim is made either explicitly or implicitly. Those propositions that claim all or none of the examples of a concept possess a characteristic assert a *uniform* claim. The statement, "All citizens of Wisconsin are also citizens of the United States," says that without exception (uniformly) that all Wisconsin citizens are alike in one respect. Those statements that claim that only some examples of a concept have a certain characteristic are *statistical* generalizations. They express a degree (specified or unspecified) of probability about the asserted relationship. The statement, "Fifty-one percent of all human births are male," is obviously statistical, and so is the claim, "College graduates earn more money during their lifetime than non-college graduates." In this latter statement there is an understood assumption that the claim is accurate for most college graduates even though there will be some exceptions. Implied but unstated is a statistical or probability claim about what is true of groups of people alike in one respect. It is common for statistical generalizations not to offer precise quantifications. Quantifiers for uniform and statistical generalizations occur through such terms as "wherever," "whenever," "always," "never," "frequently," "sometimes," "usually," "tend to," and so on as well as through specific numerical values.

Third, some generalizations express *conditional claims*, or "if . . . then" generalizations. These claims are usually, although not necessarily, considered to be assertions of causal relationships. Consider the following statement: "*If* there is an increase in the supply of a good, *then* (other things being equal) the price of that good will fall." Stated another way this proposition takes the form, "Always upon an increase in supply there is a decrease in price." Thus whether the generalization appears in uniform or conditional language a causal relationship is implied. It should be noted that all generalizations can be put in conditional form, although in some cases somewhat awkwardly, e.g., "If something is a dog, then it is four-legged."

There is a fourth general category of characteristics that generalizations can display depending on the nature of their claim. First, the claims made by these generalizations may be either *reversible* or *irreversible*. Sociology has a number of reversible propositions. For example, "If there is an increase in interaction between individuals, then there will be a greater liking for one another," and conversely, "If there is a greater liking for one another, then there will be an increase in interaction." An irreversible proposition is the following: "Whenever a man's kidneys are removed, then he dies." It does not follow that if a man dies, then his kidneys have been removed. Second, some general propositions state *necessary* conditions for an event: "If, and only if, matches are dry will they light when struck." On the other hand, some relations are described as *substitutable:* "Matches light when struck," or "Matches light when held in a flame." Third, some express *sufficient* conditions while others contain *contingent* conditions. Those expressing sufficient conditions claim an effect regardless of anything else. These are very rare and possibly nonexistent in social science. An example from the natural sciences is the following: "If a man's kidneys are removed that is sufficient for his death." On the other hand, conditions are contingent when a stated condition is able to produce an effect only if accompanied by additional conditions: "If a match is struck, then it will light, but also the match must be dry and surrounded by oxygen."

Contingent generalizations are abundant in the social sciences, but more often than not many of the contingent conditions are either unknown or assumed to be accounted for. The term *ceteris paribus* or "other things being equal" is implicit in the great bulk of social science propositions. In ordinary conversations about daily events, people state generalizations that are implicitly recognized as contingent. For instance, someone might claim that the cause of a riot was a speech delivered before an angry crowd in which they were urged to violence by the speaker. In this case the generalization could be stated as follows: "If a speaker urges a crowd to violence, then a riot will occur" (if several other necessary but unspecified conditions are also present). If the riot occurs, we will know the conditions were present, and if the prediction is inaccurate we will know that at least one of the necessary conditions was absent.

At this point it may be helpful to summarize the distinctions made so far. Listed below are the basic characteristics of generalizations covered in this section.

1. All generalizations are statements asserting a claim.
2. The claim is a relationship between examples of a concept and some specified factor.
3. Sometimes these statements of relationship are asserted in conditional form (If . . . then).
4. All these statements of relationships imply or directly state a quantification claim.
5. Quantifiers are either uniform or statistical (e.g., all, usually).
6. The nature of the claim asserted can be reversible or irreversible, necessary or substitutable, or sufficient or contingent.

These characteristics and distinctions among generalizations are useful and applicable whether they are objectively or subjectively held by individuals. A knowledge of the characteristics presented in this section is relevant to the development of social studies curriculum with both objective and subjective prerespectives. That a generalization is a unique or private insight does not exempt it from the categories discussed above. Throughout the rest of this chapter, however, we will concentrate mainly on those generalizations which are descriptive-objective in nature to facilitate our analysis. The reader should keep in mind that there are many generalizations in everyday life and language that are not the product of objective research. Subjectively held generalizations are also analyzable in terms of the variations in the claims made.

Synthetic and Analytic Generalizations

There is an additional distinction that needs to be made about the nature of generalizations. This distinction is more fundamental than those outlined above in that it deals with two different realms of knowledge served by generalizations. This difference is between those generalizations that have a *synthetic* as opposed to an *analytic* function. A generalization is synthetic when it asserts a claim about the existential world. Such claims can be confirmed or disconfirmed by some kind of empirical or evidential test. In other words, the way the "real world" is arranged makes one say "yes" or "no" to the asserted claim, e.g., "DDT is harmful to animal life." It may be, of course, that the claim is verifiable only in principle, but at least one is confronted by an assertion about the existential world that has the prospect of being tested. The following is a synthetic generalization: "None of the life forms that exists on earth is present on Venus." This general proposition is synthetic in that empirical evidence is in principle available to test this claim, if only at some time in the future. In short, a synthetic generalization can be thought of as a *synthesis of evidence* based on empirical tests.

An analytic generalization, however, is not confirmed by checking its claim against the world of nature. Analytic claims are essentially statements of how terms are used, and they describe definitional characteristics that are associated with a term. A very obvious example is the following: "All bachelors are unmarried males." This generalization asserts a necessary characteristic of bachelors and the statement is nothing more than an assertion of what is meant by bachelors.

An example of an analytic generalization from economics is the following: "Free markets are those in which price is regulated by supply and demand." This statement is definitional in that the information conveyed tells how the term is used. The term "free market" is a shorthand way of saying ". . . conditions under which supply and demand are the determinants of price." When generalizations communicate definitional characteristics for a term, it does not make sense to consider testing such statements for empirical support. Thus it is nonsensical to send out questionnaires to determine if in fact all bachelors are unmarried males. Similarly, it is not meaningful to devise tests to see if free markets are actually regulated by supply and demand. Instances of price regulation solely by supply and demand are what is *meant* by a free market.

This point may appear very obvious when made with such apparent examples, but there are numerous generalizations that at first might appear to be synthetic but in fact function as analytic. For example, "Every society has had rules, written or unwritten, by which social control over the people's conduct is maintained." [13] A first reaction might be that this is an empirical finding from research on the nature of societies and social control. Yet after analyzing the terms comprising the generalization it is difficult to avoid the conclusion that the meaning of "society" entails the concept "rules of social control." Thus, if it were found that a group of people had no rules of social control, then conceptually (definitionally) it would not be possible to call that group a society. In other words, groups of people without rules for social control can never be negative instances serving to disconfirm the generalization, since by definition such groups do not count as societies. Concepts such as society obviously have empirical referents, but one does not *discover* the nature of such concepts through empirical tests.

A final and more subtle example can be offered to illustrate the role that analytic generalizations can play in the social sciences. George Homans claims that one of the empirical (synthetic) propositions that his research has confirmed is the following: "The more a member conforms to the norms of a formal organization, the greater likelihood that he will be promoted." [14] In other words, this proposition seems to be saying that individuals who engage in activities valued by an organization will be rewarded with promotion, and that this statement is arrived at by going out into the world and taking some kind of empirical measurements.

But a close examination of the proposition reveals that the truth of the claim does *not* depend on empirical tests. Once the meanings of the terms comprising the generalization are made clear it is possible to agree with the claim without gathering any empirical evidence. The key terms in the generalization are "member," "promoted," "conforms," "norms," and "formal organization." Once the *ordinary meanings* of these terms

---

[13] James G. Womack, *Discovering the Structure of the Social Studies* (New York: Benziger Brothers, 1966), p. 3.

[14] George Homans, *The Human Group* (New York: Harcourt Brace Jovanovich, Inc., 1950), p. 141.

are spelled out it is conceptually true that formal organizations promote those who conform. How could it be otherwise? Does it make sense to say that something is a formal organization with certain norms and that those promoted are destructive to the norms? The following analysis indicates not.

To be a member of a formal organization is to accept a role which is designed to achieve the aims of the organization. Norms have been fashioned to bring about the intended objectives. Those who are unable or unwilling to fill a role by conforming to its demands and thereby achieving the goals of the organization are "misfits" and "failures." A few may succeed in an organization and not conform, but these are either leaders of emergent norms or simply those who are able to slip through the organization's evaluative criteria. It is a synthetic problem to discover what the norms of an organization are (sometimes there is a discrepancy between stated and actual norms), and also to determine what counts as evidence of conformity. One of the ways of determining the actual norms of an organization is by seeing who is promoted. Once this is known it is analytically true that those who conform are promoted. If it were a synthetic problem, then it would be necessary for sociologists to do empirical research to discover if there are formal organizations that promote those members who defy the norms of the group. But this kind of research does not seem to make much sense. The important problem is to find out what the norms of an organization are. Thus, if a university professor's role is defined as one of research and scholarly publication, a professor who understands his role should expect to perish if he does not publish. That much is axiomatic given the kind of role he occupies. It is, of course, helpful and necessary to spell out the analytic truths based on the relationship of certain concepts, but one should not confuse analytic truth with synthetic truth. The first is primarily a matter of clarifying the meaning and implications of concepts, while the latter is primarily concerned with empirical evidence.[15]

It is a synthetic matter to arrive at statements concerning the norms of an organization. One could make an empirical study that describes the particular norms of a specific organization, how they compare with other organizations, how people are evaluated, and what rewards are granted for conformity. Thus one could examine the military, insurance companies, and university faculties to determine the specific norms and mechanisms of promotion. But it is already known, it is a given based

[15] It should be apparent that the analytic and synthetic must interact. The way concepts are used and what they mean are dependent on the real world for referents; empirical research is dependent on clear meanings to obtain accurate data. This last point has received too little attention in social science research.

on the meaning of the terms formal organization, norms, and so on, that those who conform are promoted. The crucial question one needs to ask in trying to distinguish between analytic and synthetic generalizations is: "Do I need to make an empirical study to determine the truth or falsity of the statement?"

Law-Like Generalizations

It is important to be able to distinguish between analytic and synthetic generalizations because only the latter are capable of being the lawful propositions that science is searching for through the inquiry process. It is not altogether clear what constitutes a lawful regularity in either the natural or social sciences. Basically laws are claims that some phenomenon in the natural world is consistent in its behavior without respect to time or place. Thus, gravitational pull affects bodies here and on the moon, and that was as true 2000 years ago as it will be tomorrow. This criterion would suggest that most statements in the social sciences and history are not law-like (law-like meaning those propositions that have the potential to be laws even though they have not yet been given that status).

In history, for example, one finds many generalizations like the following: "By 1890 the frontier in America was closed." This statement serves to summarize various conditions and facts that are descriptive of a particular time and place. This generalization is synthetic and thus testable assuming that the concepts "frontier" and "closed" are definable in a way that permits meaningful selection of evidence. However, as stated, the proposition could not possibly offer a regularity of nature, rather it serves to summarize or colligate information about conditions in a particular context. Because of this characteristic these synthetic generalizations are often referred to as past tense generalizations.

The term "past tense" is in no way a technical or precise term, and in fact generalizations stated in present tense grammar can be summaries of past situations. Assume for the moment that one is doing research on the political structure of early Indian tribes in North America, and, after examining various tribes, the following conclusion is stated: "Decisions are made in fairly democratic fashion by a large number of chiefs." [16] This is essentially a statistical past tense generalization because it refers to a particular group over a particular time (even if unstated). In other words the grammatical tense of a statement does not determine the nature of the claim.

[16] Mindella Schultz, *Teacher's Guide for Comparative Political Systems: An Inquiry Approach* (New York: Holt, Rinehart and Winston, Inc., 1967), p. 12.

Generalizations about events at a particular time in the past are not law-like because they cannot make any claim about events beyond the particular setting to which they refer; they are bound by time and place. One characteristic of law-like statements is their timelessness. A law asserts a claim that is good for tomorrow as well as yesterday, and because they are timeless laws are stated in present tense form: e.g., "All copper expands when heated." However, as just pointed out, it is not sufficient to formulate generalizations in the present tense to obtain law-like propositions. Yet a leading text book in social studies education implies as much in the discussion of inquiry in social studies: "A generalization in its final form is usually stated in the present tense in order to facilitate wide application in all times and places." [17] Certainly the discovery of repeated patterns of relationship descriptive of the future as well as the past hangs on more than the tense of a verb.

As previously stated, the requirements for a generalization to be a law are not absolutely clear. Laws of nature essentially claim a regularity to be universal in the sense that given certain specified conditions the regularity exists without respect to time or place. Laws may be either uniform or statistical. The following is a law expressing a statistical regularity: "The half-life of radium is 1700 years (The probability is 50 percent that a particular radium atom will disintegrate within 1700 years, or 50 percent of the atoms in a piece of radium will disintegrate in 1700 years)." Much of modern science is based on probability or statistical regularities, and the notion held by some individuals in the social sciences that for a proposition to be a law it must assert a uniform regularity is untenable. It appears that virtually all empirical work in social science results in statistical statements, and for the foreseeable future any social science laws will be statistical in form.

Statistical laws are basically of two types. First, there is the *a priori* probability of mathematics which allows (with certain assumptions) the precise calculation of probability. For example, the probability of a coin coming up heads on each successive toss is ½; or the odds of drawing any spade from a deck of cards are 13/52. The second major category of statistical popositions results from quantifying the relative frequency of an event. The death rate of 30-year-old men, or the percentage of smokers as opposed to nonsmokers who develop lung cancer, is each expressed in a statistical generalization that indicates the probability that a member of the group will possess the characteristic. The statistical generalization cannot tell us if a particular member will develop cancer if he smokes, but for the population a probability figure can be offered concerning an individual's chances of getting cancer. It is the relative

[17] Massialas and Cox, *Inquiry in Social Studies*, p. 120.

frequency generalization that is of most interest in the social sciences.

In summary, there are two broad categories of knowledge: synthetic and analytic. Analytic generalizations are statements about the definitional characteristics of a concept. The truth of such generalizations is dependent upon the meaning of the terms involved—the way the language is used. Synthetic generalizations are claims about the existential world. They are dependent for their truth value on empirical evidence. Furthermore, synthetic generalizations are either law-like or non-law-like. In the latter category are all those statements referring to particular times and places. This kind of generalization is frequently found in social science and historical literature. Laws, on the other hand, assert claims applicable to the future as well as the past, and these may include a variety of characteristics including statistical claims.

Laws and Theories

Philosophers of science have devoted considerable attention to the concept of scientific law. One way to get at the nature of scientific laws, and at the same time clarify the implications of the inquiry process, is found in the analysis of Richard Braithwaite. He begins by pointing out that the only specific agreement on criteria among philosophers is that every law is a generalization. However, he argues that only those generalizations occurring in established scientific deductive systems can be called laws. For him, laws must have two kinds of support: first, empirical support in the way of evidence, and second, deductive support. The latter is obtained when a proposition is deductible from higher level generalizations in some theoretical system. It also occurs when a generalization relates theoretical terms which are in turn related to other theoretical concepts within a deductive system.[18]

Braithwaite's case of the black ravens helps clarify the implications of this position. He argues that

> the blackness of all ravens is surely "accidental" if no reasons can be given for such blackness; and this is equivalent to saying that there is no established scientific system in which the generalization appears as a consequence. If a reason can be given for the blackness of all ravens by exhibiting such a scientific system, this generalization will be regarded as lawlike.[19]

Thus even though a proposition may have considerable empirical support (every observed raven has been black) this alone is not sufficient

---

[18] Braithwaite, *Scientific Explanation,* p. 301-2.
[19] Ibid., p. 304.

for it to be called a law. The point is that lawfulness implies much more than a body of empirical support. The likelihood that the next raven one meets will be black is very high, but this represents only an isolated fact. The goal of science is to develop broad ranging theories to account for events. Isolated propositions about the blackness of ravens or any other phenomenon does not do this.

Part of the process of developing theories is constructing theoretical concepts. Carl Hempel emphasizes the role of these concepts in his discussion of laws. He indicates there are two levels of scientific inquiry: "the level of *empirical generalization,* and the level of *theory formation.*" [20] The early stages of inquiry into a subject usually result in the discovery of regularities about directly observable phenomena. These generalizations are descriptive of ordinary events such as "Wood floats in water," or "People repeat behavior they find rewarding."

At the level of theory, however, unobservable concepts are employed that provide higher level laws that account for lower level empirical propositions. The goal of theory formation is eventually to subsume a wide variety of empirical generalizations under a very few theoretical laws. Examples of unobservable or theoretical concepts are molecule, atom, ego, id, drive, status, and other terms under which a variety of directly observable behavior can be included. It is essential that theoretical concepts be developed to broaden the applicability and power of systematic inquiry. Often empirical generalizations have exceptions which cannot be accounted for until theoretical terms and laws have been formulated. Take for example these generalizations: "Wood floats in water; iron sinks in it." As they stand they have important exceptions, as when wood becomes waterlogged and when iron floats upon being given an appropriate shape. By moving to the level of theory, however, these observable generalizations and their exceptions can be taken into account by introducing a theoretical concept. In this case the concept is density which is defined as the quotient of a body's mass and volume ($D = M/V$). Using this concept the following generalization (a corollary of Archimede's principle) can be stated: "Any body floats in a fluid if its density is less than that of the fluid." One is now in a position to understand why some wood does not float and why ocean liners made of steel do not sink.

Efforts to develop theoretical concepts and generalizations in the social sciences have not been as successful as in the natural sciences. Furthermore, when social science attempts to move from low-level observational generalizations to theoretical propositions, there is a tendency

[20] Carl Hempel, *Aspects of Scientific Explanation* (New York: The Free Press, 1965), p. 178.

to come up with propositions of high probability and low information value. Such generalizations are almost certainly true in some sense but do not say anything specific about events. Sociologist George Homans refers to these propositions as *orienting statements*.[21] As an example of this kind of generalization, Homans offers the Marxian generalization that the organization of the means of production determines the other features of society.[22] Homans argues that this proposition does not specify the nature and amount of change in society resulting from a change in the means of production. At best an orienting statement allows one to say that some abstract factor is related to some other abstract factor in some unspecified way. These statements are helpful in pointing one in a direction and giving him some clues as to what to look for, but as they stand such generalizations are unable to say anything specific about the world.

In keeping with the position expressed earlier that a generalization must be part of a deductive system to be considered a law, orienting statements do not qualify as laws. In other words, propositions that express a relationship between theoretical concepts are not necessarily sufficiently informative to be considered a law, if they are not deductively related to more specific generalizations. In the final analysis, the goal of a science is to provide a body of knowledge that has high information value. In Homans' words, "sooner or later a science must actually stick its neck out and say something definite. If there is a change in *x*, what sort of change will occur in *y*? Don't just tell me there will be *some* change. Tell me *what* change." [23]

Social Science Laws

The study of human behavior and social interaction is nearly as old as the study of natural phenomena. At an earlier stage much investigation into man and society was a kind of moral philosophy rather than a systematic empirical analysis; nevertheless it seems that sufficient time and energy have been devoted to the discovery of generalizations about human behavior that some implications and conclusions can be drawn about these efforts.

Are there any laws of human behavior, and if so, what are they? These questions seem to flow naturally out of the analysis presented up to this point. Answers to these questions are really beyond the scope of this book, at least in any definitive sense, but it is possible to suggest

21 Homans, *The Nature of Social Science,* pp. 14-18.
22 Ibid., p. 14.
23 Ibid., p. 18.

several difficulties that seem to plague attempts to develop social science laws. Pointing out these difficulties will give some sense of why massive research efforts in the social sciences have not been successful in developing the powerful predictive theories that characterize some of the natural sciences.

It does not seem to be controversial to say as Ernest Nagel does that "in no area of social inquiry has a body of general laws been established, comparable with outstanding theories in the natural sciences. . . ." [24] Furthermore, it does not appear likely that a general theory of human behavior will be achieved in the near future. It may even be that *widely accepted* theories will not be available soon even in limited areas of the social sciences. For instance, attempts to develop macroeconomic theory have produced several competing versions, none of which has been able to demonstrate such clear superiority as to win general acceptance with professional economists. There are neo-Marxists, neo-Keynesians, monetarists, and so on, each with a different theoretical position designed to explain the workings of the economy. The inability of a theory, in economics or in any other area of inquiry, to gain general acceptance is due primarily to its failure to produce reliable generalizations, i.e., the inability of its generalizations to consistently account for variables and thus provide accurate predictions. It is true, of course, that controversy over competing theories also exists in the most sophisticated of natural sciences, but these controversies usually take place at the cutting edge of research and do not persist throughout the entire field as is true in the social sciences.

Despite the obvious limitations of existing social science theory, it is true, as Nagel suggests, that social inquiry has produced general relationships of dependence between certain kinds of social processes; "and these inquiries have thereby supplied more or less firmly grounded generalized assumptions for explaining many features of social life, as well as for constructing frequently effective social policies." [25] Nagel shows obvious caution in this statement by not referring to these generalizations as laws or theories.

Whether these "general relationships," as he calls them, can be developed into social theory possessing a high degree of predictive power is an open question. Nevertheless, there is enough creditability and prestige associated with several disciplines that they have become part of the policy-making apparatus in the society. It is now unthinkable for a president of the United States to make economic policy without the guidance of professional economists of one theoretical brand or another.

24 Ernest Nagel, *The Structure of Science* (New York: Harcourt Brace Jovanovich, Inc., 1961), p. 447.
25 Ibid., p. 449.

Likewise, sociological theory is becoming increasingly important in public policy. For example, sociological generalizations about the effects of segregation on the Negro were partially responsible for the Supreme Court decision declaring segregated schools unconstitutional. Politicians have come to rely upon generalizations about voting behavior in deciding their election strategies. In short, social science generalizations play an important part in the conduct of human affairs despite the difficulties encountered in developing highly reliable and generally acceptable theories.

The example of forecasting election trends based on generalizations about voting behavior brings to mind just how difficult it is to find laws of social behavior. In analyzing the generalizations offered by political scientists concerning voting behavior, it becomes apparent that there are real differences between the natural and social sciences. Typically generalizations about voting behavior state that certain racial, ethnic, economic, or special interest groups vote in highly reliable ways, and that the outcomes of elections are forecast on this information. But such generalizations cannot be interpreted to claim that there is some *lawful* connection between (say) the Democratic Party and the voting behavior of urban Negroes. A moment's reflection will show that a change in values, perceptions, or issues on the part of either the voting group or the party could invalidate the generalization. Despite the fact that voting behavior generalizations do not qualify as laws under the criteria established in the last section, they do communicate a significant level of information that permits one to make *projections*. A projection is different from a prediction in that one simply extends what has happened in the past into the future. In other words, one is saying that things will be the same if they do not change. If urban Negroes continue to see things the same way as they have in the past, they will vote as they did in the past. Such generalizations are no doubt helpful, but they do not qualify as a body of social science theory.

George Homans, an advocate of theory building in the social sciences, contends that only a few propositions have been developed that possess both the generality and high information content required of laws. Homans argues that the only law of human behavior thus far articulated by social scientists is the following: "When a response is followed by a reward (or 'reinforcement'), the frequency or probability of its recurrence increases." [26] Other propositions closely related to this one are:

> If a response is followed by a reward, the probability of that response recurring is increased.
>
> The higher the value placed on an action, the more likely it is to recur.

[26] Homans, *The Nature of Social Science,* pp. 36-37.

The more a person is deprived of a reward, the greater the value placed on that reward.

The more satiated a person becomes with a reward, the lower the value of that reward.

Frustration in obtaining a reward leads to aggressive behavior.

What it would take to develop these propositions into a full-fledged theory is not altogether clear. As they stand, these generalizations simply say that people tend to do those things they like to do and will get upset if they can't do them. This is certainly not very startling.

Homans points out that although these propositions are usually associated with learning theory in psychology, they also coincide with the theoretical framework of all the social sciences. Thus, as the various disciplines deal with decision making, a rational-choice model of man is assumed. For any given person, a rational choice is made to obtain a reward or valued goal, and the means to a goal have been calculated as likely to succeed. The difficult job for social scientists is to ascertain in given situations what it is that people find rewarding and to determine what means they will calculate to achieve the rewards.

One of the main distinctions to be made between the natural and social sciences is the difficulty the latter has had in arriving at generalizations of law-like generality and high information content. One of the reasons for this condition is the relatively greater complexity of even the most simple and ordinary kinds of social behavior.[27] The complexity factor results in the need to develop concepts and methodological apparatus that are correspondingly more complex in attempting to identify relevant variables. Greater complexity of social phenomena means that social scientists need to use more sophisticated techniques than natural scientists in their efforts to find a given level of probability and information in the regularities they formulate. It is often easy to find one or two variables that are sometimes associated with a social phenomenon, but identifying a broad range of factors for an event, and thus obtaining high probability and information value, is quite a different matter.

In contrast to the complexity that characterizes human behavior, consider the relative simplicity that an early scientist like Galileo encountered in his work in physics. In order to determine the rate at which a body naturally falls, he measured the rate at which a ball rolls down an inclined plane. Fortunately for him there was little loss of energy due to friction, air resistance, and so on. Also he was fortunate in having to work with only three variables to develop his law: distance traveled,

[27] For an interesting and readable analysis of this point see Michael Scriven, "A Possible Distinction Between Traditional Scientific Disciplines and the Study of Human Behavior" in H. Feigl and M. Scriven, eds., *Minnesota Studies in the Philosophy of Science,* Vol. 1 (Minneapolis: University of Minnesota Press, 1956).

time elapsed, and velocity. Even if there are Galileos somewhere in the social sciences, it is doubtful that their research will be as productive because of the nature of their field.

It is true that some kinds of behavior with sharply limited parameters can be regularized and predicted with high probability. These events are "simple" because the range of alternatives is very small. Certain highly controlled laboratory experiments are of this type. The situation is structured in such a way that the variables are few and responses are channeled into a predictable pattern. This is true also of some situations in daily life. For instance, one can generalize and predict quite reliably about the behavior of persons who find themselves standing in the middle of a railroad track with a train bearing down upon them. Of course, this kind of generalized knowledge does not require the efforts of social science research.

The problem of trying to relate theoretical generalizations to particular situations is acute. Take for example the following proposition: "Frustration leads to aggression." Homans suggests that this is a well-documented generalization that qualifies as law-like. But how is this generalization to be applied to particular situations? How is one to go about discovering what is frustrating to individuals in given situations? And in given situations what form will a person's aggression take? Essentially the problem is how to move beyond the vagueness and simplicity of what verge on being orienting statements to propositions that take into account the complexity of human behavior.

Implications for Curriculum

In order to see some of the implications that the nature of generalizations holds for curriculum, it is necessary to refer to the analysis in the preceding chapter regarding the four curricular perspectives. One perspective is descriptive—objective—and dominates the curriculum built on the position that it is valuable to know objective generalizations about the social world. These generalizations are objective in the sense that they claim a particular relationship exists between phenomena, and that this relationship can be verified by anyone who wishes to make the necessary inquiry. Objective generalizations are the product of a public methodology and language. The concepts comprising each statement mean essentially the same thing to all who employ them. Descriptive-objective generalizations are essential if people are to communicate about relationships in the social world.

As mentioned at the beginning of this chapter, generalizations permit one to transfer knowledge from one situation to another. Insights gained in specific and unique situations can be generalized to new contexts. The widespread transfer value of social science generalizations is dependent on their objectivity. The clearer the concepts within the generalization the more they communicate. Those disciplines with the most powerful (i.e., explanatory and predictive) generalizations have clear and precise concepts. The most powerful generalizations are those laws that hold for phenomena regardless of time or place.

Summary

It is apparent that generalizations are an important element in everyday communication as well as in more sophisticated social science or historical research. Generalizing is not something that can be avoided in a misguided attempt at scholarly objectivity. On the other hand the existence of generalizations does not necessarily mean that one is in possession of great power and insight. As pointed out early in the chapter, there are a variety of roles and functions for generalizations. Some generalizations are relatively low-level in terms of their significance, while others are relatively powerful because of their ability to explain and predict. While any social studies curriculum will include generalizations of one kind or another, it is an open question as to how much attention should be given to including law-like propositions and explanatory-predictive theory. In part, the answer to this question depends on how successful social science is in formulating reliable propositions and theories which can be translated into curriculum.

The preceding analysis calls attention to the dominant role that descriptive-objective generalizations play in formal curriculum. Clearly objective generalizations have usually been seen by educators as more significant than those that are subjectively held. More recently, however, there has been a trend to recognize the importance of subjective knowledge. Private insights and knowledge are frequently very useful to an individual, and to the extent such knowledge would be useful to others, we believe there should be an attempt to objectify that knowledge. The process of developing objective knowledge is, in fact, the movement from private insights to public verification and objectification.

The Science Model
of Explanation

5

Introduction

Before getting into a specific conception of explanation, it will be helpful to briefly consider some of the various ways "explain" and "explanation" are affected by pragmatic or contextual considerations. Jane R. Martin points out that there is a difference between explanations that are *for someone* and those that are not.[1] Any time an explanation is for someone, there is necessarily a pragmatic dimension or peculiar context which must be considered if the person receiving the explanation is to be enlightened. The pragmatic part is finding out what is puzzling to a person and determining what is needed to resolve that puzzlement. Also whenever an account is offered by someone in an effort to explain a phenomenon, the explanation has a pragmatic dimension for the explainer.

[1] Jane R. Martin, *Explaining, Understanding, and Teaching* (New York: McGraw-Hill Book Company, 1970), p. 15.

He perceives the phenomena to be of a certain type and accounts for it in the way he believes appropriate. In short, any explanation that is offered by or for someone has a pragmatic dimension.

In developing the notion of pragmatic dimension, Professor Martin indicates that at least four variations of explanation are pragmatic in some way. These variations can be expressed in the following manner:

A explains E.
A explains E to B.
X is an explanation of E given by A.
X is an explanation of E for A.[2]

In these models, A and B are persons, X is a sentence or sentences, and E is some phenomenon in question. In each of the models, a person is involved in some way with respect to the formulation, presentation, or reception of the explanation.

According to Martin, there is one conception of explanation that eliminates the pragmatic dimension. It can be stated in the form: X is an explanation of E. This indicates that there is a sentence or sentences which account for an event independent of any person. This explanation is an objective and logical construct that exists apart from any individual giver or receiver. Such explanations can be objectively evaluated because they do not depend upon any special or private conditions that are inherent in the pragmatic dimensions of the other four conceptions of explanation.

Most of the discussion in this chapter is concerned with logical rather than pragmatic considerations of explanation. It is not that pragmatic notions are less important than logical ones, but pragmatic factors by definition are concerned with particular and peculiar contextual matters. Except at a very abstract level it is difficult to anticipate and generalize about the various particular problems that givers and receivers of explanations will face.

In order to clarify her analysis of explaining something to someone, Professor Martin outlines what she believes to be the essential pragmatic requirements for the acts of explaining.[3] These requirements can be summarized as follows:

1. The question in need of explanation can be answered.
2. The explainer understands the question in the sense it was asked.
3. The person asking the question understands the nature of the question.
4. The explainer states the right answer in the process of explaining.

2 Ibid., p. 19.
3 Ibid., pp. 128-29.

5. The explainer also provides subsidiary explanations that are needed to account for the primary question.
6. The explainer facilitates reasoning and judgmental operations on the part of the questioner.
7. At the end of the episode the explainer has organized and stated the answers required for (3) and (5).

This analysis appears to be fairly noncontroversial in that most people would agree that good explainers do take these factors into consideration whether consciously or not. At the same time, however, these characteristics have been abstracted to a point where they are of little help in developing particular explanations. One can agree that these characteristics are important, but how do they help develop frameworks around which explanations can be built? In other words, what model could one use to provide a framework to achieve a satisfactory explanation? One of the goals of this book is to show that there are different models and kinds of explanation. These differences arise out of the nature of various questions that are asked with respect to different kinds of puzzlements.

In the broadest sense an explanation is a response to almost any question asking for clarification of a puzzling situation. To explain is to fill in the gap that exists in someone's knowledge as a result of answering an explanation-seeking question. Thus one can explain how something is done, why someone acted as he did, what happened, what the meaning of something is, when or where something took place, who is responsible for an act, why an event occurred, and so on.[4] A key factor in explaining is to find out what question was asked and then respond in a way that supplies the information needed to fill a knowledge gap. The first part of this task is a practical or pragmatic problem of sensing the nature of the perplexity, and the second part is logical and empirical. The next section of this chapter will develop a single logical model (deductive) which facilitates a particular kind of explanation (scientific).

Scientific Explanation

A scientific explanation is a response to a particular kind of question or puzzlement. The term scientific is not meant to be an honorific title bestowed on some form of explanation to indicate its superiority to other explanations. Rather the term scientific is a descriptive title given to those explanations that meet certain logical and empirical requirements. Scientific explanations are responses to questions that seek to find out why a particular phenomenon occurred in the sense that the

---

[4] For a thorough logical analysis of the various aspects of explanation, see Robert H. Ennis, *Logic in Teaching* (Englewood Cliffs, N.J.: Prentice-Hall, Inc., 1969).

phenomenon is an instance of a known regularity. For instance, someone may ask, "Why are astronauts weightless in space?" Or in symbolic terms, the question takes the form, "Why is it the case that *p?*" Here the questioner is asking for an account that shows the phenomenon (*p*) of weightlessness in space is something to be expected given certain laws. By describing the empirical conditions of space travel it is possible to logically deduce the case of weightlessness from the known laws about gravitational pull.

Like other explanations, a scientific explanation has a pragmatic dimension when it is given by or for someone. In other words, the pragmatic dimension consists of a necessity to determine whether this kind of explanation is an appropriate response to the question asked. For instance, the question might be asked, "Why was there a revolution in America in 1776?" The pragmatic problem in this case is to determine if the question is actually a request for an explanation of the kind that shows an event to be deducible from a regularity. Is it appropriate from the standpoint of the questioner that his question be put in the form, "Why is it the case that *p?*" It might be that the questioner wants, or at least prefers, an explanation of another kind, such as an account of the events leading up to the revolution. It may be that the questioner is not sure about the kind of response he wants, or even that he doesn't know there are alternative ways to explain the revolution.

In any case, once one gets beyond the pragmatic dimension and decides to offer a scientific explanation for some event the concern shifts to logical and empirical problems. The logical concern is with developing a syllogism in which the event in question (*p*) is deduced from a law-like generalization or general law. A classic example is the following: "All men are mortal, Socrates is a man, therefore Socrates is mortal." Essentially a syllogism is an argument in which two premises necessitate a conclusion. Arguments are characterized as either valid or invalid. The premises of a syllogism can be verified as either true or false (more or less) by empirical tests. The conclusion in a deductive argument must be true if the premises are verified and the reasoning is valid.

Most scientific explanations are more complex than simply deducing an event from a single general law. Most events have complex conditions surrounding them and usually several laws are required in the course of an explanation. Carl Hempel, in a discussion about the nature of scientific explanation, recounts a case that represents more accurately actual explanatory situations and arguments. He relates that John Dewey, while washing dishes one day, observed the following phenomenon:

> Having removed some glass tumblers from the hot suds and placed them upside down on a plate, he noticed that soap bubbles emerged from under

the tumbler's rims, grew for a while, came to a standstill and finally receded into the tumblers. Why did this happen? Dewey outlines an explanation to this effect: Transferring the tumblers to the plate, he had
trapped cool air in them; that air was gradually warmed by the glass,
which initially had a temperature of the hot suds. This led to an increase
in the volume of the trapped air, and thus to an expansion of the soap
film that had formed between the plate and the tumbler's rim. But gradually, the glass cooled off, and so did the air inside, and as a result, the soap
bubbles receded.[5]

Although Hempel's account of Dewey's explanatory argument is stated
informally, it is possible to show the event in question as a conclusion
to a deductive argument whose premises contain general laws.

In the above situation the particular conditions accompanying the
event were: the tumblers had been immersed in soapsuds of a higher
temperature than the surrounding air; the tumblers were placed upside
down over a puddle of soapy water, and so on. The set of regularities
can be expressed through gas laws, and other laws involving heat ex-
change between bodies of different temperatures.

The formal model of scientific explanation that expresses the relationship between the conditions, laws, and event to be explained is dia-
grammed in the following manner: [6]

$$C_1, C_2, \ldots, C_k \quad \text{(conditions)}$$
$$L_1, L_2, \ldots, L_r \quad \text{(laws)}$$
$$\overline{ E } \quad \text{(event or } p \text{ to be explained)}$$

This diagram shows that the conditions together with the laws permit
one to explain an event through deduction. The conditions describe the
boundaries of the event in question, and the laws express general regularities for events of that type. The event is a particular phenomenon
which is shown to be an instance of more general regularities of law-like
nature.

If any of the laws in the deductive argument is statistical, then the
event (E) is not strictly deducible. Instead the conclusion of the argument will be no more than probably true. A probable explanation is, of
course, compatible with the nonoccurrence of that event. This has led
some individuals to take the view that scientific explanation can be
achieved only when the conclusion is shown to be the necessary consequence of the argument, that individual cases are the important ones,

---

[5] Carl Hempel, *Aspects of Scientific Explanation* (New York: The Free Press,
1965), pp. 335-36.
[6] This schema is a slight modification of the one offered by Hempel in ibid., p.
336.

and that if individual events are not strictly deducible then no scientific explanation is possible.

However, this position is difficult to maintain in light of the fact that many accepted explanations in the natural sciences make explicit use of statistical laws that permit only probable conclusions.[7] For example, in physics the entire field of quantum mechanics is essentially statistical, and yet very accurate explanations and predictions are conspicuous features of this field. Another example is found in genetics. Based on Mendelian principles it can be predicted with very high probability that a sample of pea plants whose parents are a cross between white-flowered and red-flowered plants will be approximately 75 percent red-flowered and the rest white-flowered. The point is that scientific explanations are developed around statistical premises. While the conclusion is not strictly deducible, the conclusion is implied with the certainty expressed by the degree of probability in the law or laws. Probabilistic explanations can be every bit as informative as strictly deductive accounts when it comes to groups or populations of events.

A major contention of this book is that these two variations of scientific explanation are basic to the natural sciences. Most inquiry and research in the natural sciences is aimed at explaining particular events by showing them to be subsumed under general uniformities of either uniform or statistical type.

A number of well-known social scientists have adopted this view of explanation in accounting for social phenomena. David Easton, Hans Zetterberg, and George Homans have construed their research in terms of developing scientific explanations for social events.[8] For instance, Homans argues that the success of a science can be judged by its ability to provide explanations. To him, the term explanation means the "special sense of explaining why under given conditions a particular phenomenon occurs and not in one of the vaguer senses in which we use the word." [9] He goes on to say that this special sense of the term means to deduce the event in question from generalizations. Thus for Homans the model of explanation attributed to the natural sciences also serves the social sciences.

It would seem that if one is to understand what many social scientists are trying to do, it is essential to have a clear understanding of scientific

[7] For further clarification of this point see Hempel, *Scientific Explanation,* pp. 376-80.

[8] David Easton, *The Political System* (New York: Alfred A. Knopf, Inc., 1953); Hans Zetterberg, *On Theory and Verification in Sociology* (New York: Bedminster Press, 1965); George Homans, *The Nature of Social Science* (New York: Harcourt Brace Jovanovich, Inc., 1967).

[9] Homans, *The Nature of Social Science,* pp. 22-23.

explanation. This model holds a number of implications for those developing curriculum, and in the next section several of these are explored.

Structure and Scientific Explanation

It has been pointed out that many social scientists accept scientific explanation as the goal of their inquiry, and implicitly they are willing to have the success of their inquiry judged in terms of its ability to provide these explanations. If scientific explanation is the goal of inquiry, then it follows that a prerequisite of this goal is the development of law-like generalizations and theories. *These two logical elements, along with precise concepts, are the structural components which enable one to organize empirical evidence into scientific explanations.* The notion that these structural components lead to scientific explanation is something that has not been previously clarified by those who are concerned with the development of structure within social studies curriculum.

Much has been said in the literature about structure, usually referred to as "structure of the discipline," but little has been done to clarify the point that the capstone of structure is scientific explanation, at least for those inquiries that accept the basic assumptions of the science model of inquiry. Jerome Bruner has defined structure as the underlying principles of a discipline.[10] This, of course, is not very helpful unless we have some criteria for determining when an underlying principle has been found. Joseph Schwab has offered an analysis of structure that provides some detailed criteria helpful to those in the social studies. He suggests three elements as the basis for the structure of a discipline.

First, Schwab says there is "the body of imposed conceptions which define the investigated subject matter of that discipline and control its inquiries." [11] Imposed conceptions, or simply concepts, are any of the categories developed within particular disciplines to focus inquiry. Concepts serve to pull from the mass of available data certain pieces of evidence that are useful in inquiry. For example, "gross national product" and "status" are concepts from economics and sociology that are used to describe certain phenomena. The greater discriminatory power provided by a concept the more precise the inquiry can be.

The second element in Schwab's analysis of structure is syntax. The syntactical element is the pattern of a discipline's procedures, "its method, how it goes about using its conceptions to attain its goal." [12]

---

[10] Jerome Bruner, *The Process of Education* (Cambridge, Mass.: Harvard University Press, 1960), pp. 17-26.
[11] Joseph Schwab, "The Concept of·the Structure of a Discipline," *The Educational Record,* 43 (July, 1962), 199.
[12] Ibid., p. 203.

In other words, syntax is concerned with the manner in which the discipline moves from raw data to its conclusions.

It is obvious that disciplines such as algebra and history use radically different data but it may not be so apparent that they also have dissimilar methods of verification. History and algebra have recognized ways of warranting conclusions that belong to those disciplines. In other words, "proof" means something different in each area. The goal of these disciplines has much to do with their syntax. A discipline that has the goal of producing interrelated logical systems has a different syntax than a discipline attempting to produce singular empirical conclusions. The first goal can be ascribed to algebra, and the latter goal is characteristic of history. In neither case, however, is the syntax designed to produce what has been described as scientific explanations.

Schwab's third aspect of structure is the substantive element. The substance of a discipline is the body of confirmed knowledge that the concepts and syntax have discovered in the course of inquiry. Substantive conclusions include singular statements, generalizations, and theories. These are the products or warranted findings of empirical inquiry.

Schwab takes the position that the goal of inquiry in the *sciences* is the discovery of substantive principles of both greater validity and scope. Principles of greater validity are achieved when they "embrace more and more of the richness and complexity of the subject under investigation." [13] Principles of wider scope are those embracing "a wider and wider range of subject matters, which will reduce what were before considered as separate and different phenomena to related aspects of a common kind or source." [14]

The importance of discovering substantive principles (law-like generalizations) of some validity and scope is that they function as connecting patterns of relationship between phenomena. As pointed out in the previous chapter, a related system of generalizations is a theory. Theories are important because they broaden and enrich the tested and reliable patterns of relationship between phenomena. Broad and rich theories are particularly powerful in their ability to explain and predict events. From this viewpoint, explanation and prediction are two sides of the same coin. These two operations result from the structure that provides the empirical requirements for the model of scientific explanation. The success of inquiry can be judged by the reliability of the structure it produces. Good inquiry is that which produces structure that successfully predicts and explains phenomena.

It is apparent from any examination of the literature on inquiry and

[13] Ibid., p. 201.
[14] Ibid., p. 201.

structure in the social studies that the role of scientific explanation has not been clarified. The result of this situation has had its effects on curriculum development. As pointed out in Chapter 1, there has been great concern with identifying particular concepts and generalizations to be taught and/or discovered, but curriculum materials are woefully weak in showing how structural components are part of the inquiry process that leads to scientific explanations. To the extent one wants to design a curriculum that focuses on objective explanations of the world, then the science model is appropriate as a foundation. It is inconsistent, or at least incomplete, to emphasize structure and inquiry process in a curriculum without also including the intended theoretical goal of these logical elements.

Scientific Explanation in History

In 1942 Carl Hempel published an article entitled "The Function of General Laws in History," [15] and the analysis he presented at that time has served as a catalyst for a continuing lively discussion on the nature of explanation in history. Hempel's argument is considered the classic statement of the view that scientific explanation *should* play an indispensable role in historical inquiry. Most of those who investigate the nature of explanation in history have felt compelled to comment on the Hempelian position in some way. Before examining some of this discussion, a brief look will be taken at Hempel's position as he has developed it.

Hempel begins with the assumption that human behavior is part of an objective unity of nature, i.e., human behavior is not essentially different from the behavior of other natural phenomena. Man is part of nature and his actions can be studied in the same way and with the same goals found in other sciences. He argues that the function of law-like generalizations is the same in both the natural and social sciences, with history being a member of the latter. As already presented, the function of laws is to provide the basis for scientific explanations, but history as it is usually written leaves the laws implicit in the course of the narratives. Unstated and undeveloped laws and deductive arguments lie behind the explanations historians offer.

The explanations historians offer are usually what Hempel calls an *explanation sketch*.[16] These sketches consist of a more or less vague

---

[15] The original article appeared in *The Journal of Philosophy*, 39 (1942), 35-48. A slightly modified version has been reprinted in *Aspects of Scientific Explanation*, pp. 231-43.

[16] Hempel, "General Laws in History," p. 238.

indication of the conditions and laws that are needed to develop a scientific explanation. Hempel sees an explanation sketch in need of "filling out" so that it can be stated as a syllogistic argument. The laws employed in such deductions are not necessarily historical laws in the sense that they are the product of inquiry by historians, for explanatory laws may be drawn from any discipline that has discovered regularities. Thus Hempel is not arguing that historians must discover their own laws, or that peculiarly historical laws are lurking behind historical explanations. Hempel's position is simply that when one looks behind explanations offered by historians he will find implicit regularities and deductive arguments, even if historians do not intend them.

One misinterpretation of Hempel's position is found in the view that an historical event is explained by "covering" it with a law.[17] In fact Hempel's position is sometimes referred to as the "covering law" thesis. Taken to its logical conclusion this view sees any event that historians might wish to explain being subsumed under *a* law. Thus William Dray describes a situation in which a car's engine stops running because a hole in the oil pan has allowed the oil to run out.[18] Dray, in attempting to attack Hempel's position, correctly argues that there is no law which covers a situation in which a hole in the crankcase is followed by engine failure. It would seem absurd to attempt to maintain that complex events are ever covered by a single law. In the case of the oil leak and engine seizure, it would be necessary to employ several laws regarding motion, friction, heat, and the expansion of metal in order to explain this phenomenon. There is no doubt that physicists can explain this phenomenon to their own satisfaction by means of several laws.

Dray's use of the term "covering law" is unfortunate because of what it seems to imply. The term suggests that an individual law somehow encompasses a specific event no matter how complex that event is. On the face of it this is illogical. Most social events are very complex, and in fact the more complex they become the more likely they are to be the focus of explanation. Furthermore, laws express relationships between theoretical types of phenomena. Laws do not refer to vague complex situations, such as engine failures or the emergence and recession of soap bubbles around tumblers. Instead laws include general factors which have been conceived from and applied to a wide variety of phenomena manifested in particular cases. Laws are readily transferrable in the sense that those which help explain the failure of an engine without oil also explain why the water in a car's radiator becomes hot, why the

17 William Dray, *Laws and Explanation in History* (New York: Oxford University Press, 1957). Dray uses the term "covering law" throughout this and several other works.
18 Ibid., pp. 66ff.

wings of a supersonic jet are warmed rather than cooled from the air rushing by, and why a person can warm his hands by rubbing them together briskly.

If one looks at laws as statements about the relationship between types of events, then the process of developing an explanation requires that specific events be described in terms of types of events that have some theoretical relationship. Some ordinary language descriptions of types of events have no theoretical relationship. Ordinary language frequently fails to make necessary distinctions or fails to recognize the similarities between phenomena. For example, a car radiator can crack if it contains water and the temperature falls below freezing, or it can crack from overheating, or from a flaw in the metal, or from a sharp blow. It appears fruitless to search for a "radiator-cracking law," since this term does not refer to a type of event, at least for the purposes of science. What is fruitful is to develop concepts and descriptions of those types of events possessing theoretical relationships which can explain various cracked radiators. In short, it is necessary to isolate relevant factors in terms of precise concepts that distinguish between various types of events. These can then be developed into scientific explanations.

The problem remains, however, to develop the precise concepts that define the conditions for a type of event. A case that points out the difficulty in identifying these conditions is one that Hempel uses to illustrate the nature of historians' explanation sketches. Hempel uses an historical situation involving the movement of farmers from the drought-stricken areas of the midwest to California during the 1930s. He quotes an historian to the effect that in the 'thirties, farmers from the Dust Bowl migrated to California because of the continued drought in their states, and because they had a vision of a better life in California. According to the Hempelian position, behind a statement of this kind is a tacit assumption of at least one law-like generalization. In this case he suggests that the "explanation rests on some such universal hypothesis as that populations will tend to migrate to regions which offer better living conditions." [19]

Certainly the causal statement that farmers migrated because of the drought and a vision of a better life appeals to our common sense. On the other hand, the "law" that populations tend to migrate to regions which offer better living conditions is full of problems. There is a host of factors that must be taken into account before reasonably precise statements can be developed to describe this type of event. A set of precise concepts would permit the development of a law or laws only if the following questions are answered: What are the conditions and

[19] Hempel, "General Laws in History," pp. 236-37.

how severe must they be before people become sufficiently dissatisfied to consider moving to a new place? What are the necessary conditions to facilitate a migration? Must there be some precipitating event that touches off the movement with respect to individuals in the migration? Certainly there are various restraints that could prevent a migration (e.g., the Berlin Wall). What is the nature of these restraints? Can they be psychological as well as physical? What kinds of information or myth are necessary to promote the view that another area offers a "better life"? These and other questions need to be systematically answered based on the power of general laws, before one can begin to explain and predict particular migrations. It is this kind of elaboration and filling out that is necessary before explanation sketches can become scientific explanations.

Two conclusions should be emphasized about the use of scientific explanation in history. First, it seems clear that complex events cannot be explained (or "covered" in Dray's sense of the term) with a single law. Second, to develop laws one must be able to describe types of events in terms of precise concepts that can account for the relevant condition that bears upon an event. These two points are consistent with the emphasis in the last chapter placed on the development of theories or related deductive-empirical systems that provide the explanatory law-like generalizations. One does not, in other words, develop scientific explanations for historical events by putting in generalization form the existing causal language offered by historians to describe an historical event.

This point is significant in that it warns against attempts to convert causal statements directly into laws.[20] These statements should be viewed instead as claims that, given sufficient elaboration, supplementation, and development of conditions and concepts, laws can be developed to provide a scientific explanation of an event. Usually causal statements in history are not just inadequately or incompletely stated laws and scientific explanations, but rather they are guideposts to mark the place where deductive arguments need to be developed. These are the points at which theoretical knowledge needs to be applied.

An understanding of this has some practical considerations. It helps to clarify the rather limited nature of many causal claims in history, i.e., limited from the standpoint of scientific explanation. Historians, for example, in making causal claims about events are not committing themselves to the position of being able to formulate scientific explanations for those events. If an historian says he knows the cause of an event, he is not necessarily saying that his "cause" is essentially a law-like generalization. Thus, for example, Frederick Jackson Turner has made

---

[20] Morton White, *Foundations of Historical Knowledge* (New York: Harper and Row, Publishers, 1965), pp. 59-65.

causal statements to the effect that the presence of a frontier gave rise to democracy; Charles Beard has made causal statements to the effect that the presence of farmers and debtors was responsible for the development of democracy. Some critics have attempted to destroy such arguments by claiming they directly imply law-like generalizations. In effect, the critics assumed that these causal statements, which were actually past tense generalizations about particular situations, implied laws that claimed *whenever* there is a frontier, or *whenever* there are farmers and debtors, then there will be democracy. Such generalizations, if they are intended to be law-like, would seem to be superficial, and it is questionable whether Beard and Turner saw them functioning this way.[21]

Trying to figure out what an historian intended with his statements is really not the problem, however, because if one accepts the goal of trying to develop scientific explanations for historical events, then causal claims in history become signals that an opportunity exists for a scientific explanation. In other words, if an historian makes causal statements about the relationship between events or conditions, there may be gold to be mined at that spot for those interested in scientific explanation. From the standpoint of explanation, most written history can be seen as the preliminary spadework for attempts to develop a different kind of knowledge. By filling in the essential logical elements, scientific accounts can replace the imprecise but not necessarily inaccurate statements by historians.

The Curriculum and Scientific Explanation

The previous section was devoted to considering the role of scientific explanation in history, but nothing has been said about its role in the social sciences. The authors assume that those who have followed the analysis presented thus far can readily see the role of scientific explanation in the social sciences; these disciplines are conceived in the image of natural science with its successful use of the science model. The social sciences have as their goal the discovery of concepts, generalizations, and theories that can be used to deductively explain social phenomena. In terms of curriculum, these logical elements can be the substantive content of the social studies. One can simply teach them as the structures of the various disciplines, or employ them to explain phenomena in the course of examining social problems.

This last point has a particularly important implication for curriculum. Those developing curriculum and teaching strategies should keep in mind that the structural elements of a theory or discipline need not

---

[21] See Lee Benson, *Turner and Beard* (New York: The Free Press, 1960).

be taught in the abstract. Often the notion of teaching the structure of a discipline is conceived in terms of learning a set of concepts and generalizations apart from real human problems. It is not unusual for a "principles of . . ." course to have students learning material that seems divorced from reality. If one keeps in mind that theoretical knowledge is significant if it can be applied, and the success of application can be measured in terms of its ability to provide explanations for human questions, then there is no reason to see theoretical knowledge as somehow irrelevant. For example, a student can learn something of the concepts and generalizations of sociological theory as he attempts to explain the riot in Watts, the rise of a radical student movement, or the causes of revolution.

The above examples can be described in terms of their historical development, and this is certainly a legitimate context in which to place them, but they can also be explained with social science theory. The scientific explanation of events requires, of course, that theoretical knowledge of some reliability be available for application. A crucial question is to what extent are there law-like generalizations and theories already tested by the various disciplines that will permit one to develop this kind of explanation. In the previous chapter some doubts were raised about the availability of such knowledge.

Turning to the field of history, it can be useful to look at the explanation sketches offered in text books to see how these sketches might be developed to provide scientific explanations. Consider the following account offered by a popular high school text as an explanation for the phenomenon of revolution:

> Throughout modern history, however, revolutions have usually occurred among people who were relatively well off rather than among those who were the most miserable and oppressed. Generally, it is not misery itself that brings about revolt. Rather, it is the contrast between actual and ideal conditions. When the experiences of a people cause them to expect more than they have been given—or to fear the loss of what they already possess—they are ripe for revolutionary discontent. If they have enough energy, education, resources, and political skill, they may act upon their discontent by organizing themselves and launching a revolution.[22]

This series of universal generalizations is not typical of historical writing. Although the statements are qualified and hedged, historians are usually reluctant to make these kinds of claims, at least explicitly. This particular example does serve to illustrate, however, that the basis for law-like generalizations and scientific explanation does exist in historical

22 Richard Current, Alexander De Conde, and Harris L. Dante, *United States History* (Glenview, Ill.: Scott, Foresman and Company, 1967), p. 44.

accounts. As it stands, the above paragraph is only the outline of a more fully developed explanation of human behavior. A series of questions would have to be answered in the development of full-fledged scientific explanations for revolutionary situations. Thus, why is it that people relatively well off do revolt, and why is it not the case that the more miserable people become, the more likely they are to revolt? What are the necessary conditions for people to see a gap between actual and ideal conditions? Which gaps between which conditions are productive of a revolutionary movement? Certainly not every unfulfilled ideal produces a revolutionary movement. And what does it mean to say that "enough" energy, education, resources, and political skill are needed to promote the revolution? Clearly the above account is an explanation sketch that needs to be filled in with theoretical knowledge from the social sciences before a scientific explanation of the American or any other revolution can be offered. Particularly relevant would be theories from social psychology as well as more conventional material from political science and comparative history.

Causal statements like those in the above example offer an opportunity to fill in broad and comprehensive theories. As indicated, however, historians are not usually engaged in trying to offer sweeping accounts for events in general. They are ordinarily concerned with a particular revolution and its causes. Nevertheless, any time an historian makes a causal claim about an event, he is offering an explanation sketch even if the language used in the account is not specifically couched in terms of cause. The following example taken from a high school text is offered to show that even in the course of the most ordinary narrative, historians do assume generalizations about human behavior and that these assumptions could be elaborated into a full-fledged scientific explanation.

The open range and the roving cowboy made an exciting and important contribution to the taming of the West, but their days were numbered. Railroads crept nearer and nearer to the home ranches. When contagious cattle diseases broke out, cattlemen were prevented by quarantine laws from moving their herds from one section to another. Sheep raisers and homesteaders, who followed the railways into the plains, fenced in feeding areas and waterholes so that the cattle could no longer graze at will. Public demand for more tender meat led to the breeding of better beef cattle than the long-legged, open-range steer—but such animals were too valuable to risk to the hazards of the hard winters. Great fenced-in ranches, operated as big businesses, began to supply the meat-packing companies. In the 1890's few cattlemen depended entirely on the open range, but instead grew winter feed for their cattle.[23]

23 Leon H. Canfield and Howard B. Wilder, *The Making of Modern America* (New York: Houghton Mifflin Company, 1954), p. 349.

Nowhere in this paragraph is the term "cause" used, but clearly a series of causal relations is more or less directly assumed. These various causal relations can be analyzed in terms of the theory that would fill them out. For example: As the railroads crept nearer the ranches, there was no need for cowboys to make long drives (if there is no demand for a skill, then that skill will disappear). As contagious cattle diseases broke out, the cattle could not be moved across the open range (if men are threatened with economic loss, then they will seek strategies to prevent that loss). As the range and water holes were fenced in by sheep raisers and homesteaders, the open range was reduced for cattle (if there is an increasing demand for goods with a fixed supply, then those goods will be depleted). As better cattle were bred, they replaced the open-range steer (if there is demand for a new product, then there will be a decline in the demand for the old product). These presumably law-like generalizations can be shown to be part of basic economic theory dealing with the concepts of supply, demand, price, and market.

The generalizations cited are in one sense trivial, i.e., one was already aware of them and they are learned just by living. These are truisms which lie behind many of our everyday or common sense explanations of events.[24] Thus any attempt to spell out in detail the theoretical nature of the several causal assumptions in any particular portion of a narrative may not add much to someone's store of knowledge, unless it would be to expose the fallacies in apparently obvious kinds of statements. In pointing out that even the most ordinary kinds of narratives contain causal relations, the authors are not suggesting that every such historical account *should* be unpacked for its theoretical implications. This would be an endless task and would quickly result in a proliferation of triviality. Rather it is the teachers and the curriculum builders along with the students who must make decisons about what causal relationships are worth investigating in terms of scientific explanation. These decisions can be made in part on the basis of student and teacher interests and also in part on the basis of available explanatory theory. This last point should be noted because it is doubtful that students could be expected to develop new theories even under the guidance of the most skillful inductive teaching. Students can, of course, be expected to learn (or discover) theoretical material, but the goal should then be to have them apply this knowledge to questions they have about the world.

At the risk of being repetitious, we wish to remind the reader of a number of assumptions lying behind what is said in this chapter. First, a discussion of scientific explanation makes sense only if one assumes

---

[24] Michael Scriven, "Truisms as the Grounds for Historical Explanations," in Patrick Gardiner, ed., *Theories of History* (New York: The Free Press, 1959), pp. 443-75.

that there are objective regularities in human behavior. Second, objective regularities are law-like and permit one to develop objective explanations for people's actions. And third, curriculum should provide instruction in the nature of the inquiry that provides this knowledge, and should give students an opportunity to inquire into real questions about social phenomena.

If one has the goal of getting students to provide scientific explanations for genuine questions about social phenomena, then one of the teacher's roles is to help students make the theoretical work of academicians relevant to particular problems in the real world. The social studies teacher occupies a creative role by helping translate and apply what sometimes appears as irrelevant and needlessly abstract work by those in the disciplines. The task of translating and applying theoretical knowledge can be carried out at various levels of sophistication and thoroughness. The teacher's job is to assess the level of competence in the classroom and help students move beyond the level of story telling, myth making, factual regurgitation, or even the discussion of controversial issues when this is done without explanatory knowledge.

Most of the social studies curricula that have been developed in recent years ignore the logical roles of concepts, generalizations, and theory in developing scientific explanations. Lists of concepts and generalizations are provided but without any apparent role in explaining social phenomena. In addition, theories are generally ignored as somehow apart from concepts and generalizations. In fact, of course, these logical elements become really useful only when they are put into a larger theoretical framework. The explanation of events is a logical goal for curricula that emphasize the learning of concepts and generalizations. By focusing on explanation rather than concepts and generalizations the dichotomy that some have seen between a problem or issue centered curriculum and a structure centered curriculum is dissolved. Teaching the structure of a discipline without application to real problems and social issues is inadequate and lacks significance for many students. On the other hand, an issue-centered curriculum, if it is to have any depth, must provide opportunities to base choices and values on the best available knowledge. A key aspect of this knowledge is being able to utilize that which is predictive and explanatory. In short, the issue-structure dichotomy in curriculum is a false one; not only are these two approaches to curriculum compatible but also mutually supportive.

Up to this point the tone of this chapter has been very positive in terms of utilizing the model of scientific explanation to account for events, whether these events be construed as history, contemporary issues, or something from one of the social sciences. Regardless of the way events are construed, the argument has been that they are in principle explainable with the deductive model through the use of law-like generalizations. Of course, it is obvious that without sound theory no scientific explanations can be achieved. A crucial question that must be asked, then, concerns the availability of the necessary law-like generalizations. Are the social sciences able to offer reasonably tight theories that go beyond the mere categorization and description of events? Have the social sciences succeeded in developing law-like generalizations to the point where they are really useful in explaining and predicting events? In the previous chapter on generalizations, some doubts about the status of social science generalizations were raised.

If the answers to these questions are negative, then the preceding analysis of the role of scientific explanation is not very helpful. Moreover, if one takes the position that the prospects of social science achieving explanatory-predictive theory are not bright, that little or no progress in theory development will take place, then the notion of scientific explanation of social events is absolutely irrelevant.

Those who find little explanatory substance available in the social sciences, and hold that such power is not likely to be available in the future, are saying that the meaning of "explain" is quite different for human and social behavior than it is for natural phenomena studied in the sciences. Since the use of "explain" is quite common in history and social science, there must then be an alternative to the science model. To explain the actions of men in society must mean something other than to deduce those actions from regularities. Human behavior needs to be accounted for in some other way and the study of such behavior is conceptually different from the model developed by the natural sciences. The next chapter offers an alternative to scientific explanation.

Summary

The science model of explanation has had considerable impact on the development of contemporary thought. The deductive form is both aesthetically pleasing and logically precise. The success of the natural sciences has led social scientists to seek the same kind of explanatory-predictive power. Clearly a comprehensive science of human behavior would provide highly interesting, useful, and dangerous knowledge. An important question for the social studies concerns the extent to which curriculum should be devoted to the science model of explanation. In part, an answer depends on the extent to which such explanations can be developed by professional social scientists and historians. If the level of theory development remains either trivial or imprecise so that only truisms or vague conclusions are deduced, then probably little attention can be given to scientific explanation.

An Alternative View
of Explanation

6

In the last chapter, an analysis of scientific explanation was presented along with some of the implications this kind of explanation holds for social studies curriculum. The emphasis in that chapter was on a descriptive-objective form of explanation. This chapter presents both another model and another kind of explanation utilizing this model. This alternative view of explanation permits one to deal not only with descriptive-objective knowledge but also descriptive-subjective knowledge. In addition, it permits one to deal with valuative-objective and -subjective judgments.

The first section deals with an alternative to the deductive model—known as the narrative model—which is explanatory in a variety of contexts. The second and third sections of this chapter deal with a different conception of what it means to explain. A kind of explanation different from scientific explanation is developed. This alternative conception springs from different assumptions about the kind of information that explains human behavior. A main thrust of this chapter is to indicate that there is more than one way to explain, and when it comes to human behavior, scientific explanation in and of itself is not necessarily satisfactory.

Scientific explanation is conceived as an objective form and is not concerned with the unique psychological aspects surrounding a person's request for an explanation. Thus if one asks a question in the form, "Why is it the case that *p*?" one ought to be satisfied if it is shown that the instance in question ("Why do steel ships float?") is deducible from the general law that all bodies float if their specific gravity is less than the fluid in which they are immersed. If the person requesting the explanation went on to say that he knows about the general law and he sees that the phenomenon in question is subsumed under it, but that he still wants to know why steel ships float, then the person offering the explanation would be at a loss to know what would be considered explanatory. Once certain assumptions behind the system of science are embraced there is a logical answer to questions about what is a satisfactory explanation.

While the science model of deductive explanation is explanatory in those areas where there are general laws under which phenomena in question can be subsumed, there is a wide variety of situations in which there are no general laws to cite. Moreover there are many situations in which people simply do not expect or want to be given this kind of explanation. It ought to be apparent that any explanation to be satisfactory must remove the puzzlement of the questioner. If a person asks the kind of question that requires a scientific explanation in the deductive form, then nothing else will do. If another kind of explanation-seeking question is asked, again nothing other than the kind of explanation that is psychologically satisfying will do. Explanation-seeking questions arise out of what a person knows and what he wants to know, and some of the questions people ask do not intend to elicit deductive arguments. In short, there are different kinds of questions that seek a variety of responses which can be labeled explanations.

Almost any kind of (true, accurate) response can qualify as explanatory if it meets the particular needs of an individual by removing his puzzlement. Even a single word or gesture can be explanatory given a particular gap in a person's knowledge or understanding. This means that in a given situation an explanation may be satisfying to one person and not to another. An account may be unintelligible to one person and quite understandable to another. Also a question may elicit a response which is understandable, but it is inadequate in providing the kind of explanatory knowledge that the questioner is seeking. In other words, in the last analysis the adequacy of explanations is closely tied to subjective or personal considerations for their adequacy.

Explanations are objective when the ground rules for what counts as an explanation have been clarified and agreed upon by a group or public. If one is asking a question that seeks to know under what regularity a particular phenomenon can be subsumed, then a scientific explanation is being requested. Such explanations have objective standards for their adequacy: (1) The evidence and logic of these explanations are independent of any particular individual who tests or applies them. (2) The reliability of the general law under which a phenomenon is subsumed is publicly verifiable. Thus the question, "Why do satellites orbit the earth?" can be answered by means of well-established empirical and logical relationships.

On the other hand, the question, "What caused the Civil War?" has no publicly agreed upon set of standards to establish an objective answer. Is this question asking that the Civil War be subsumed under a general law? If the intention is to obtain a scientific explanation for this question, it must be shown that events of this type are instances of some regularity in the nature of human affairs. Many historians, however, reject this meaning for the question and instead see the need to trace the development of a series of unique events that led up to the Civil War. Others might reasonably interpret the question as asking for the motives of people who were involved in the decisions and activities of that time. In other words, why did people do what they did, i.e., go to war? Each of these interpretations of the question is conceptually different and requires a different kind of explanatory response. Moreover, in answering the question in the sense of why did people do what they did, there is a wide range of potentially credible responses. There are many possible histories that can explain the causes of the Civil War. There may be better and worse history but there is no public set of standards for explanations in response to questions of the type being considered here. History is constantly being revised in part because there is no objective (agreed upon) method of determining when historians have adequately answered a question. The question about why satellites orbit the earth has been objectively answered and will remain so unless and until there is a conceptual revolution in the way physicists look at the world.[1]

Many of the explanations that people typically offer in daily affairs require them to make subjective decisions about what qualifies as an

---

[1] Thomas Kuhn, *The Structure of Scientific Revolutions* (Chicago: University of Chicago Press, 1970).

adequate account. For example, if someone is asked to explain why he voted the way he did, or why he made a certain remark to his neighbor, there is no objective set of standards for determining the adequacy of the explanation offered. The person receiving the explanation will have to make a personal decision on the credibility of the account. This is not to say there are no standards by which to judge an explanation of this kind, but they are loose enough to permit one to refer to such explanations as being essentially subjective, at least when one compares them on a continuum with scientific explanation. This should not be seen as a comparison between scientific explanation and a less objective one. It is simply a matter of recognizing that there are different kinds of questions which require different kinds of responses.

The Narrative Model

Many different questions are requests for explanations, but there is one kind of question that is typically asked by historians, social scientists, and also by laymen in ordinary affairs. Generally it takes either of these forms: "What happened?" or "How did it happen?" While it may be possible to distinguish between these two questions, the answers usually take the same form—a narrative or story.

The narrative is essentially a story that purports to delineate the birth and growth of an event or the development of a situation or condition. Narratives are always sequential, cumulative, and they always lead to some conclusion. Biologists, geologists, psychologists, and historians in the course of their work all trace an event or condition over time from some point of origin to a terminus, at which point the event or condition is said to be explained. Each of the following questions typically asked by historians and social scientists can be answered by developing a narrative: "How did the king gain ascendency over the nobles?" "What caused the riot in Watts?" "What led to the stock market crash of 1929?"

It is possible to answer these questions by telling how the situation in question came to be, i.e., how it happened that one thing led to another until the event in question took place. It is almost always the case that when someone asks, "What happened?" he can be satisfied by some story that has as its conclusion an event or condition that served to originally raise the question. If a police officer, for instance, investigating the scene of an auto accident asks what happened and is told that an accident took place, understandably he might say with some impatience that he can see as much and he wants to know how and why it happened. He wants a story of the accident. Arthur Danto offers the following narrative as an explanation that could satisfy the question asked by the officer:

> The car was driving East behind a truck; the truck veered left; the driver of the car thought the truck was making a left turn, and proceeded to pass on the right; but the truck then sharply veered to the right, for it had gone left to make a difficult right turn into an intersection which the driver of the car had not seen; and so there was a collision.[2]

While this account may be incomplete in the sense that more details need to be included before the officer will be satisfied, the narrative does offer an explanation. It could be an adequate explanation—assuming of course that the statements are accurate. To the extent that some of the statements are not objectively verifiable some people would find the account inadequate or unsatisfying.

The logic of the narrative is in the way it relates data to reach a conclusion. A narrative constantly provokes the question, "And then what happened?" For someone to understand the story, the narrator must show how the events and conditions go together, how they have some significance and relevance to each other in arriving at a terminus. It is the narrator's job to present all of the relevant information needed to provide transitions from one point to another as the story unfolds.

William Dray, who describes the narrative as the "model of the continuous series," emphasizes the need to trace the course of events over time.[3] Thus if the narrative is presenting an individual's reasoning about a course of action, the reader must be able to follow the logic of the actor as he arrives at his conclusion. Similarly if a narrative is designed to show how a series of events led to some conclusion, the reader must be able to see the connections, i.e., see how one thing led to another. The narrative form is capable of presenting a wide variety of explanations and the adequacy of a particular narrative is in the final analysis dependent upon what a person knows, what he wants to know, and what new insights the account is able to offer.

This relativistic approach to judging the adequacy of a narrative does not mean there are no standards of a general nature that can be applied to accounts. Arthur Danto has suggested three general criteria that a narrative should meet before it can be said to offer an explanation in ordinary affairs, history, or social science.[4] First, a narrative should tell what actually took place over a period of time. Unlike narratives found in literature, history and social science narratives should offer a "true" rather than a fictional account of what happened. Second, the person receiving the narrative must be able to know the order in which events

---

[2] Arthur Danto, *Analytical Philosophy of History* (New York: Cambridge University Press, 1965), p. 202.

[3] William Dray, *Laws and Explanation in History* (New York: Oxford University Press, 1957), pp. 66-72.

[4] Danto, *Analytical Philosophy*, pp. 112-42.

occurred. An account that do
Party came before or after
offering an adequate expl
is significant about a sul
do not bear on the con
do bear upon the concl
these conditions expla
pened, in the order i

An interesting po
and the narrative mc
that many scientific ex
points out that Hempei,
tive model of explanation, i.
scientific explanation in narrative fo.
of John Dewey's explanation of the soap
receded around some tumblers he was washing:

part of an historian's or
siderable agreement th
it is probably not co
place—they are part
scientists, and the
on Pearl Harbo
November 22
phrases are
other even
what bro
relatio
came
an

> Why did this happen? Dewey outlines an explanation to u.
> Transferring the tumblers to the plate, he had trapped cool air in th.
> that air was gradually warmed by the glass, which initially had a tempera-
> ture of the hot suds. This led to an increase in the volume of the trapped
> air, and thus to an expansion of the soap film that had formed between
> the plate and the tumblers' rims. But gradually, the glass cooled off, and
> so did the air inside, and as a result, the soap bubbles receded.[5]

This explanation as it appears here takes the form of a narrative; it
tells what happened, in the order it happened, and presumably includes
the significant factors. These "significant factors" are what make this
account a potential scientific explanation because they imply that deductive arguments can be constructed. In short, part of the significance of
the narrative in this case is the inclusion of factors that can be combined
into general laws. Thus given the right kind of knowledge one can move
from a narrative form into a deductive form of explanation. The point
is that the narrative form can be explanatory in the sciences as well as
in history and the social sciences.

The most difficult part in developing a narrative is deciding what is
significant and what is not. In the sciences an explanatory account is
significant to the degree that it is objective and employs concepts and
generalizations that explain and predict. In history and the social sciences, however, statements within a narrative explanation that purport
to show a link between two events or conditions are often controversial
because they tend to be subjective in nature. This is the interpretive

[5] Carl Hempel, *Aspects of Scientific Explanation* (New York: The Free Press,
1965), pp. 335-36.

social scientist's work. There is, of course, con-
certain specific events did occur. For example,
ntroversial to say that the following events took
of the objective knowledge held by historians, social
lay public: the stock market crash of 1929; the attack
, December 7, 1941; the assassination of John F. Kennedy,
1963. These events are in one sense "facts," but these
nsignificant as they stand because they are not related to
s. One wants to know what is significant about these events,
ught them about, what consequences did they have, and what
ships existed among the human actions that went before and
after these events. In order to give events significance, historians
social scientists develop narratives which tell what happened over
me. They must show how these events are linked to other events.

A key question concerns the way in which narratives are constructed.
How does one go about developing a narrative? It is apparent that given
the stock market crash of 1929, for example, one could develop an
infinite number of stories about that event. By its very nature any narrative would have to leave out much more than it included, and the
person constructing the account must have some way of selecting what
is to be included. The narrator must impose some boundaries on his
task. He must begin with certain assumptions, hunches, and questions
that define his task. He does this only by imposing some kind of hypo-
thetical framework on the available data. His hypothesis provides criteria to accept some things and reject others. Those events which fit the
hypothesis are included in the story of what happened. The heart of
this hypothesis is the question or questions to be answered by the narrative. The nature of a question determines the direction of the narrative.
The questions are based on hunches that shape the narrative by seeking
only certain data that can provide answers; data which do not help
answer a question are not included in the explanation. The significance
of events arises out of the way they provide answers to questions. The
hypothesis and hence the narrative is a conception of the way events
can be put together to answer questions.

It may seem heretical to claim that historians and social scientists
impose a preconception on their data to help determine what is significant. This is heresy in view of the argument advanced by some
that the essence of objectivity is to refrain from imposing preconceptions
on empirical evidence and thereby to let the evidence speak for itself.
Objectivity is thus associated with an absence of any framework that
allows a person to select some things and reject others, since an act of
selecting and rejecting is thought to be a subjective one. The notion
that objective accounts come out of the data itself is a holdover from

the strong Baconian tradition that has influenced empiricism in Western Society, stating that "true induction" is the basis of objective science. Preconceptions will only result in distorting the facts from what they actually are.

For example, Charles Beard, a strong proponent of the Baconian view, maintained that if history was to be scientific the historian must approach his work without preconceived theories.[6] Any overarching hypothesis about events under study would move the historian away from "history-as-actuality." To be scientific the historian must eliminate any subjective element that would distort objective reality. But this view is untenable for both history and science. The nature of inquiry is inseparably tied to the testing of hypotheses and theories. While the nature of hypotheses and theories may differ between history and science, both areas need frameworks within which to organize data. Neither area can avoid the use of hypotheses. In the case of history and social science, the hypothesis in a narrative form of explanation arises out of the question asked and the proposed answer that satisfies that question.

There is a basic difficulty with the view that preconceived frameworks for selecting data result in an inherently subjective explanation. It seems doubtful that individuals can develop explanations without coming to their data with a variety of preconceptions, assumptions, and biases which impinge on their analysis. This means that subjective factors do help shape the hypotheses established in the process of inquiry. This is true of both the historian's narrative and the physicist's laboratory experiment. All inquiry is subjective in this sense, but the crucial factor is the degree to which the results of an inquiry can be intersubjectively criticized. Explanations that arise out of hypotheses imposed on data can be publicly testable to some extent. The notion of an intersubjective or public test for knowledge is possible because there are agreed-upon standards that the knowledge must meet before a public is satisfied. Explanations that adequately answer (publicly satisfy) questions raised about phenomena can be called objective.

In some areas of inquiry there is more agreement as to what the standards are than in others. Historians have only general rules about evidence and the use of sources. Physicists have a more precise and specific set of standards revolving around explanation, prediction, and reliability of results in addition to the usual rules of evidence. If it can be said that an historian's narrative is not as objective as the report of a physicist's experiment, it is not that the former has somehow destroyed the objectivity of his work by imposing a hypothesis on the data while the latter has somehow avoided this, but rather the degree of

[6] Danto, *Analytical Philosophy*, pp. 101-2.

objectivity each obtains is determined by the publicly testable nature of the procedures and knowledge presented.

Typical scholarly historical works take the form of a narrative or series of narratives. Historians offer interpretations in their narratives and their goal is to offer more adequate interpretations by basing their accounts on refined or original hypotheses. There is constant revision in the field of history because it is always possible to come up with a slightly different hypothesis and then go about selecting data that are relevant to it. There is almost always considerable empirical warrant for what historians say in their interpretations, i.e., the evidence they offer in their interpretations supports the hypothesis in question. The difficulty is that historians frequently disagree with the assumptions of a particular hypothesis or find enough contradictory evidence to support competing hypotheses. For major historical events there is an infinite number of possible narratives that could be constructed. The criteria of objectivity in history (and frequently in social science also) are not sufficiently available or agreed upon to provide narratives that are relatively noncontroversial.

To illustrate the points that have been made thus far about the narrative form, an example is presented and followed by a brief analysis. The example has been deliberately chosen from biology rather than history or any of the social sciences as a way of demonstrating that (1) the narrative is considered explanatory within the natural sciences, and (2) that to the extent there is no objective test for a conclusion there will be competing hypotheses and narratives to explain a phenomenon. Note that in this case the narrative begins with an explanation-seeking question.

> Why should the amphibians have developed these limbs and become potential land-dwellers? Not to breathe air, for that could be done by merely coming to the surface of the pool. Not because they were driven out in search of food, for they were fish-eating types for which there was little food on land. Not to escape enemies, for they were among the largest animals of the streams and pools of that day. The development of limbs and the consequent ability to live on land seem, paradoxically, to have been adaptations for remaining in the water, and true land life seems to have been, so to speak, only the result of a happy accident. . . .
>
> The Devonian, the period in which the amphibians originated, was a time of seasonal droughts. At times the streams would cease to flow. . . . If the water dried up altogether and did not soon return, . . . the amphibian, with his newly-developed land limbs, could crawl out of the shrunken pool, walk up or down the stream bed or overland and reach another pool where he might take up his aquatic existence again.
>
> Once this development of limbs had taken place, however, it is not hard to imagine how true land life eventually resulted. Instead of immediately taking to the water again, the amphibian might learn to linger about the drying pools and devour stranded fish. Insects were already

present and would afford the beginnings of a diet for a land form. Later, plants were taken up as a source of food supply. . . . Finally, through these various developments, a land fauna would have been established.[7]

To answer the question, "Why should the amphibians have developed these limbs and become potential land-dwellers?" a narrative is developed that takes into account various known data as well as inferences from the data. Sentences linked in the form of a story were put together in such a way that the phenomena in question (development of limbs and becoming land-dwellers) were explained. The narrative tells what happened, in the order it happened, and tells the significance of what happened. The narrator takes such data as "the Devonian was a time of droughts," and makes inferences that supplies of insects and foliage encouraged the development of land fauna, and then he relates these statements into an account which presumably tells what happened, in the order it happened, leaving out nothing significant. While the narrative does explain the phenomena in question, it seems apparent that there are a number of other potentially explanatory hypotheses that could be developed about the same general situation. In other words, the story is convincing but not irrefutable.

Frequently natural scientists are able to come up with more than one hypothesis to explain certain facts, and the competing explanations can be equally convincing. A classic case is the extinction of the dinosaur. Given the available data it is possible to construct several alternative and plausible accounts of why the dinosaur became extinct. This kind of problem is even more prevalent in history and the social sciences. It is often possible for historians, for instance, to offer several competing versions concerning the causes of the Civil War. The complexity of the situation provides the basis for a number of competing hypotheses and narratives to explain the events surrounding the Civil War. Whether it is a biologist trying to explain the extinction of the dinosaur or an historian trying to explain the Civil War, both must settle for accounts that are subjective in an important way. Until there is some means of getting agreement on how to test alternative conclusions, by definition there can be no objective answers to many of the questions in history and social science.

The Rational Model: Explaining "Why" in History

It does not seem controversial to say that historians and social scientists, as well as the man on the street, are all interested in explaining human behavior. How they go about developing such explanations, what

---

[7] Alfred S. Romer, *Man and the Vertebrates*, 3rd ed. (Chicago: University of Chicago Press, 1941), pp. 47-48. Used by permission of the publisher.

information is needed, and how they decide that a given account is in fact explanatory are problems that involve considerable controversy. If it is assumed there are important, nontrivial regularities in human behavior, then the deductive scientific explanation can be basic in explaining human actions. Implicit in this approach to explanation is the need to find law-like generalizations stating behavioral regularities, and these general laws will in turn be used in deductive arguments that show the behaviors in question to be instances of known regularities expressed in the laws. Theory building, as discussed in Chapter 4, is the goal of such inquiry.

Many historians, social scientists, and philosophers reject the appropriateness of the science model and its assumptions when it comes to explaining human behavior. For instance, William Dray does not believe historians should be interested in scientific explanation even (and he is skeptical about the possibility) if it were possible to explain human actions with this form. His main argument is that scientific explanation is not an appropriate conceptual response to the kinds of "why" questions historians typically ask.[8]

The kind of question that underlies the historian's work is humanistic and not scientific in nature. Historians want to know the purposes, motives, intentions and reasons behind the human actions that comprise the historian's account of the past. They want to understand man as a thinking, feeling, rational, and irrational being in order to make him understandable to their readers. Man as an actor-agent in human affairs is interesting because of the uniquely human qualities that characterize his behavior. Such behavior is more than the observable movements, noises, and physical objects associated with human actions.

Dray states that "what drives us to the study of history . . . is a humane curiosity; an interest in discovering and imaginatively reconstructing the life of people at other times and places. To discover and understand their life . . . we need to take a view of them, as R. G. Collingwood might have put it, *from the inside.*"[9] In other words, the humanistic historian wants to discover the reasons, motives, intentions and purposes that form the core of these actions called history. The fundamental assumption in the humanist position is that human behavior is essentially purposeful. Correspondingly this assumption rejects the view that human behavior is explained in any meaningful sense by showing it to be instances of lawful regularity.

The historian-philosopher R. G. Collingwood argues that the observa-

8 William Dray, "The Historical Explanation of Actions Reconsidered," in Sidney Hook, ed., *Philosophy and History* (New York: New York University Press, 1963), pp. 132.
9 Dray, "Historical Explanation," pp. 132-33.

tion of external events or physical acts, which are basic to objective and hence scientific explanation, is unimportant unless it leads one to understand the *reasons* for such actions. For Collingwood, the study of the past is meaningful only through the recreation of experiences by re-enacting the thoughts within those experiences. Collingwood contends that the historian's task is the following:

> So the historian of politics or warfare, presented with an account of certain actions done by Julius Caesar, tries to understand these actions, that is discover what thoughts in Caesar's mind determined him to do them. This implies envisaging for himself the situation in which Caesar stood, and thinking for himself what Caesar thought about the situation and the possible ways of dealing with it. The history of thought, and therefore all history, is the re-enactment of past thought in the historian's own mind.[10]

In arriving at a recreation of some historical actor's thought, the historian is describing *what* was thought. To tell what someone thought is to explain *why* he acted as he did. Thus Collingwood is advocating a different kind of explanation for history from that typically found in the natural sciences. It is different in the sense that it has different goals: The two kinds of explanation represent different kinds of knowledge.

If one accepts the arguments of Collingwood, then it is clear that some historians are misguided in their attempts to imitate the methods and inquiry goals of the natural sciences.[11] This imitation of the so-called hard sciences is compelling because of the great success achieved in the areas of physics and chemistry; however, the relative paucity of reliable theoretical systems coming from the social sciences suggests that this imitation has serious limitations. Collingwood states directly that the science model of explanation is conceptually wrong for history:

> The thesis which I shall maintain is that the science of human nature was a false attempt—falsified by the analogy of natural science—to understand the mind itself, and that, whereas the right way of investigating nature is

[10] R. G. Collingwood, *The Idea of History* (New York: Oxford University Press, 1956), p. 215.

[11] Lee Benson, "Middle Period Historiography: What Is To Be Done?" in George A. Billias and Gerald N. Grob, eds., *American History in Retrospect and Prospect* (New York: The Free Press, 1971), pp. 154-90. In this paper Benson points out that in the first seven decades of this century more scholarly man years have been devoted to his particular area of specialization, the United States from 1816 to 1860, than any other area of specialty, American or non-American. Yet it is Benson's judgment that the value of the total scholarly product from this effort can not be defended in terms of the intellectual resources expended. He argues that the irrelevancy of this scholarship is due to a narrow conception of history that rejects the goal of theoretical knowledge of the type sought by the natural and social sciences.

by the methods called scientific, the right way of investigating the mind is by the methods of history.[12]

Fundamental to Collingwood's position is that there is a significant difference between human behavior and natural phenomena. The latter can be systematized and explained by general laws, while the former is not amenable to this approach. Thus, for Collingwood, the goals of science are conceptually empty when they are applied to the study of human behavior.

To explain human actions, Collingwood argues, one must penetrate to the inside of those actions. Human actions are essentially different from natural phenomena because it is necessary to differentiate between the outside and inside of human events or actions. The outside is the observable part of a behavior. The inside is the purpose or thought behind it. The natural scientist is rightly concerned with the observable behavior of phenomena because that is all there is for him to work with. It is absurd to conceive of natural phenomena as having an inside or a mind that man could somehow come to know.

In history, the outside of an event is the physical aspect of an action: throwing the tea overboard into Boston Harbor, or the precipitous fall of stock prices in 1929. These are both historical events described in terms of their outsides. The inside of each event would be concerned with the rationale behind the outward behavior. Thus, the motives of those participating in the Boston Tea Party, or the thinking going on inside the heads of investors and speculators as they began to sell off their stocks in 1929 would be the inside of these events. The historian, by the very nature of his profession, is interested in both aspects of an event, and, in being interested in the inside of an event, goes beyond the work of the scientist and enters a conceptually different realm.

In pointing to an inside of events, Collingwood is emphasizing the uniquely human quality of actions. Actions are unique because they occur in peculiar context-bound situations that are in part the creation of the individual doing the acting. Contexts are defined by persons as they subjectively bring their perceptions, beliefs, values, and purposes to bear on the world around them. It is these elements that go into the "thought" inside an action, and it is the historian's job to recreate contexts in such a way that he can reenact and thus understand and transmit the thought of particular actors. It is this position that led Collingwood to make the now frequently quoted statement, "All history is the history of thought." [13] By this he meant that the historian writing history had the job of recreating the thinking behind the readily visible events under

12 Collingwood, *The Idea of History*, p. 209.
13 Ibid., p. 215.

investigation. To arrive at this thought he must recreate the life and times surrounding the observable events to such an extent that he can reenact the thinking that moved men to act. The historian must immerse himself in the empirical evidence and discover what happened. The goal of understanding an actor's thought does not in any sense weaken or eliminate the role of empirical evidence in writing history. On the contrary it requires the most careful involvement of the historian with his evidence, but the data themselves are not the inside of the event. The historian must make inferences from the data about the thought that constitutes the inside of an event.

If, for example, someone is writing about Caesar crossing the Rubicon, the historian must start with the outside of this event, and then he must try to recreate Caesar's thoughts as the situation developed. What alternatives were open to him and which did he consider? What did he hope to achieve by his actions? How did he weigh the possible consequences? What peculiar perspective did he have? These and other questions need to be answered to understand Caesar's action. The empirical evidence will not directly tell the answers, and thus the historian must engage in a creative and subjective act of imagination and inference. By immersing himself in the context under study, and by coming to know the principal actors so well that he can think as they thought, the historian is able to go beyond the empirical evidence of the event.

Collingwood repeatedly points out that historians should not rely on empirical evidence as an authority that necessarily justifies particular conclusions. Anyone familiar with historical research knows that the evidence is often contradictory or inconsistent, and it is always incomplete in some sense. Thus historians must criticize their data in developing accounts that penetrate to the inside of events. Collingwood gives an example of this criticism of data in noting that Suetonius is on record as claiming that Nero once considered withdrawing his troops from Britain. Collingwood rejects this supposedly authoritative and objective evidence because he cannot incorporate this assertion of thought into a coherent picture of Nero's thought.[14] To accommodate Suetonius' statement would disrupt a coherent and understandable picture that Collingwood has carefully developed in the process of recreating the inside of certain events. For Collingwood, the final authority is not some piece of evidence that has the stamp of authority, but rather the historian's own judgment as to what makes an understandable recreation of thought and thereby gives meaning to human behavior.

Clearly this position is strongly subjective. The process of getting inside the head of another individual to discover his thoughts probably

[14] Ibid., pp. 244-45.

has better and worse methods, but it is doubtful whether there can be any procedure that does not produce largely subjective results. The conclusions from this kind of inquiry tend to be subjective in that each historian based on his unique experiences and perspectives works the personalities and events of the time into different accounts. There may be agreements on the purposes behind certain actions, but frequently each historian will explain human behaviors in different terms because each will have unique insights into the actors. There is no objective means for eliminating variations in historians' accounts. There is no corollary to scientists' criteria of explanation and prediction.

The fundamental assumption behind the position being described is that human behavior is goal-directed, and that behind actions lie purposes—more or less explicit in the mind of the agents. People behave as they do because they are trying to achieve some end. The means to that end are the actions historians try to decipher. Explanations are not some added logical and empirical formula beyond the agent's thought. To tell *what* someone thought is to tell *why* he acted as he did, and there is nothing further to explain. In a passage that has been the source of much comment by Collingwood's critics, he states, "After the historian has ascertained the facts, there is no further process of inquiring into their causes. When he knows what happened, he already knows why it happened." [15] To be able to recreate the thought of an actor is to understand that thought, and if the historian understands the thought, then he knows the "why" of the action. Thus, if an historian asks, "Why did Brutus stab Caesar?" the answer to this question is found in the thinking (rationale and justification) of Brutus. In short, to look for a cause is to look for a reason.

A sample of Collingwood's own inquiry might be helpful at this point. The following is an explanation he developed to account for an old Roman wall that was found in England.

> For example, the many archaeologists who had worked at the Roman Wall between Tyne and Solway had never, I found, seriously asked themselves what it was for. Vaguely, you could of course call it a frontier defence, and say that it was to keep out the tribes beyond it. But that will no more satisfy the historian than it will satisfy an engineer if you tell him that a marine engine is to drive a ship. How did it work? Was it meant to work, for example, like a town-wall, from the top of which defenders repelled attacks? Several obvious features about it make it quite impossible that any Roman soldier should ever have meant to use it in that way. No one seemed to have noticed this before; but when I pointed it out in 1921 every one who was interested in the subject admitted that it was so, and my counter-suggestion that the wall was meant for an 'elevated sentry walk' was generally accepted.

15 Ibid., p. 214.

A question answered causes another question to arise. If the Wall was a sentry-walk, elevated from the ground and provided (no doubt) with a parapet to protect the sentries against sniping, the same sentry-walk must have continued down the Cumberland coast, beyond Bowness-on-Solway, in order to keep watch on vessels moving in the estuary; for it would have been very easy for raiders to sail across and land at any unguarded point between Bowness and St. Bee's Head. But there the sentry-walk need not be elevated, for sniping was not to be feared. There ought, therefore, to be a chain of towers, not connected by a wall but otherwise resembling those on the Wall, stretching down that coast. The question was, did such towers exist?

Search in old archaeological publications showed that towers of exactly the right kind had been found; but their existence had been forgotten, as generally happens with things whose purpose is not understood.[16]

Here is a clear example of rational explanation. A condition is explained by showing the purpose behind it. Empirical evidence is essential for the explanation, but the key factor in developing the account is inferring motive from human activity.

The kind of inquiry found in this example calls for assessment and appraisal of action. This assessment calls for a judgment as to the reasons that are commensurate with an action. The historian must look at an action and show it was appropriate for the agent in his context. It must be shown that an action was, as Dray says, "the thing to have done." [17] This does not mean that the historian thinks the action was the intelligent or moral thing to have done, or that most people would have acted in the same way, but rather given the viewpoint, knowledge and purpose of the actor, it was the thing he should have done. In other words, if an action is purposive, there is a calculation that can be made to show why an actor did what he did. To calculate an actor's reasons one need not assume the actor recited his reasons aloud or silently. Human purpose is more subtle than this in many situations. However, if an action springs from motive and purpose, there is a calculation that can be given for that action. It is not necessarily the publicly stated rationale since it is well known that there are stated reasons and real reasons. Instead the calculation is the one the actor would give to himself if he were to recreate the situation. In short, this kind of inquiry produces "rational" explanations of human behavior.[18] Here the term "rational" is used in a broad sense to indicate a class or kind of explanation; rational explanations are essentially different from scientific explanations. These explanations do not describe or logically show some

---

16 R. G. Collingwood, *An Autobiography* (Oxford: The Clarendon Press, 1939), pp. 128-29. Used by permission of the publisher.

17 Dray, *Laws and Explanation in History,* p. 124.

18 Ibid., pp. 123-24.

behavior as rational in some objective sense, but rather it is shown that a behavior or action was the thing to have done from the subjective viewpoint of the actor.

Rational explanations are incompatible with attempts to explain behavior with law-like generalizations, which is the goal of much inquiry in the social and behavioral sciences. A rational explanation asserts a principle of action that was appropriate for an individual in a given context. Thus if a person A did thing X in situation Y because his purpose was P, the person offering the explanation does not claim that there is a *class* of A's that always or at least probably do X's in Y's. Rational explanations need not arise out of any set of regularities about human behavior in general. On the other hand, rational explanation is not the result of insufficient knowledge in the field of psychology, but rather a desire to understand an action from the subjective position of the agent.

Rational explanations have a strong foundation in the standing presumption that people act for sufficient reason. If an action appears to be extremely odd or without reason, then one is interested in discovering in what way that behavior was appropriate for the actor. In fact, it is the unusual behavior that tends to attract one to this kind of explanation. In trying to explain odd behavior one searches for odd or mistaken beliefs about a situation, or some peculiar perspective or purpose that led the person to behave in an unexpected way. More ordinary and usual behavior often is explicitly left unexplained because there is an assumption that the reasons for it are understood without further description or comment.

So far, the argument concerning the adequacy of rational explanations has focused almost entirely on the behavior of individual agents. A legitimate question concerns the ability of this kind of explanation to account for group or generalized phenomena. In other words, can rational accounts provide satisfactory explanations of the French Revolution, the westward migration to the New World, or the development of the civil rights movement in the United States? It is, after all, such general phenomena that serve as the basis of many historical problems.

Collingwood argues that generalized phenomena can always be reduced to the purposive acts of individuals. Thus group or mass behavior is in principle no different from individual actions. The job of the historian is to get at the reasons of individuals, and when he finds similar reasons among many persons resulting in similar behavior, or even when he finds that different reasons result in the same kind of behavior, he is in a position to explain a generalization. This is quite different from the science model of explanation that seeks to use generalizations to explain particular phenomena. In the case of rational explanation, a generalized behavior is noted (the westward migration from the Old

World to the New World), and then accounts are developed for why groups of people engaged in similar actions. Thus generalizations play an important role in rational explanation, and frequently that role is to be the focus of inquiry—the thing to be explained. Generalizations from this viewpoint are never laws of human behavior, but instead they are summaries of unique but also in some respects similar actions which are in need of explanation. Those engaged in offering rational explanations are very much interested in generalizations, but for the historian generalizations have a different role than for the scientist because the goals of the two are not the same.[19]

Finally, it should be pointed out that rational explanations, which have a particular goal based on a particular kind of knowledge about human action, are ordinarily presented in the narrative form. Narratives that present rational explanations tell what happened, in the order it happened, and leave out nothing significant. The criterion for what is significant is that which answers the question, "Why should X have acted the way he (they) did?" This question calls for an assessment of an action in terms of its appropriateness for the actor. As indicated earlier, the hypothesis of a narrative is formed around an answer to a question about a particular context. In the case of rational explanations, questions focus on the purpose behind behavior. In telling the "what happened" of a narrative, the historian selects data that reconstruct purpose and perception. He is able to shape his story by looking for evidence that will produce a narrative containing a rational explanation.

In summary, an alternative to scientific explanation is rational explanation, and an alternative to the deductive form is the narrative form. Scientific explanations must be able to conform to the deductive model. Rational explanations ordinarily appear in narrative form.

The Rational Model: Explaining "Why" in the Social Sciences

The arguments just presented concerning the nature of rational explanations may seem appropriate for the discipline of history, but it may seem that such explanations are inappropriate for the social sciences, that social scientists are engaged in pursuing a different kind of knowledge not found in rational explanations. In short, social scientists are the counterpart of natural scientists and the goal of both is scientific explanation. The social sciences may not be as advanced as, say, physics, but it can certainly be argued that social scientists in the course of their

---

[19] For a discussion of the various ways in which historians develop and use generalizations which are non-law-like, see Louis Gottschalk, ed., *Generalization in the Writing of History* (Chicago: University of Chicago Press, 1963).

inquiry have developed some regularities about human behavior. Moreover, there is an assumption behind much social science research that gradually there will develop a body of tested theory (similar to that already present in the natural sciences) to explain and predict.

The authors do not intend to argue that there are no law-like regularities in the social sciences, or that in principle it will never be possible to find regularities in human behavior that can be systematized into explanatory theory. Instead we intend to show that much of what is considered explanatory in the social sciences is consistent with a conception of explanation very similar to the rational explanation used by historians. There are many explanations in the social sciences that offer an assessment of human actions in terms of purposes, values, and perceptions.[20]

Social scientists offer explanations of this type from two vantage points. First, they explain why people act the way they do because of perceived means and ends. This is similar to the notion of rational explanation presented in the previous section. Second, social scientists (and historians too) explain the relationship between people's perceptions and the unintended or unperceived consequences of their actions. In an effort to illustrate this thesis, it is helpful to examine several of the social sciences to see how they offer explanations by a rational assessment of behavior. It will be clear by our examples that social scientists do not always offer scientific explanations for human behavior.

Anthropology serves as a good starting point because this discipline is most obviously concerned with the assessment of human purpose. Typically the anthropologist who sets out to inquire into the nature of another culture must begin by steeping himself in that culture. He must immerse himself in his object of study. His goal of absorbing a culture is similar to the goal that Collingwood sets for the historian. The anthropologist often tries to live the life of those under investigation. He comes to know their language, customs, values, hopes, and fears. He understands, for example, the rituals and behaviors of the Dobuans with respect to the yams, their main source of food, because he understands what they believe about magical spirits controlling the fate of the yams.[21]

---

[20] A more detailed analysis of this fundamental position concerning the philosophy of social science can be found in the following works: A. R. Louch, *Explanation and Human Action* (Berkeley: University of California Press, 1966); Charles Taylor, *The Explanation of Behaviour* (London: Routledge and Kegan Paul, Ltd., 1964); Richard Taylor, *Action and Purpose* (Englewood Cliffs, N.J.: Prentice-Hall, Inc., 1966); and Peter Winch, *The Idea of a Social Science* (London: Routledge and Kegan Paul, Ltd., 1958).

[21] Ruth Benedict, *Patterns of Culture* (New York: New American Library, Inc., 1959), pp. 121-55.

Dobuan behavior makes sense and can be explained in terms of the perceptions and purposes of the culture. This kind of anthropological research has both a subjective and an objective dimension. One must be able to "get under the skin" of those in another culture; ideally it is possible to sense the subtleties of personality produced by the culture. In describing and communicating about the culture it is, of course, necessary to have objective data. Accounts about a culture must be based on data that are available and understandable for anyone equipped to do the same research.

Describing the cultural characteristics of people different from oneself is a legitimate goal as it stands. However, some philosophers and anthropologists have argued that out of such inquiry must eventually come law-like generalizations and theories that explain and predict. Anthropology has not been particularly successful in developing scientific explanations because, in the view of the writers, most of the behavior being studied is value based in the *final analysis*. The anthropologist uses such concepts as convention, function, status, and role in formulating his research about the nature of human behavior in a particular society at a particular time. Each of these concepts guides the researcher in his assessment of means and ends for people. Thus these concepts have at their root the notion of obeying cultural prescriptions or instructions, doing the job or tasks assigned by the culture, and in general playing one's part in the scheme of things. When a person's behavior is said to be role-fulfilling, then an assessment has been offered which says that particular behavior is appropriate for the cultural role. In making this kind of judgment one makes a valuative statement in the sense that given the requirements of a particular role, the observed behavior was the right thing to do.

To illustrate the point being made here consider the analysis Ruth Benedict offers for the Kwakiutl Indian culture.

> The ultimate reason why a man of the Northwest Coast cared about the nobility titles, the wealth, the crests and the prerogatives lays bare the mainspring of their culture: they used them in a contest in which they sought to shame their rivals. Each individual according to his means, constantly vied with all others to out-distance them in distributions of property. The boy who had just received his first gift of property selected another youth to receive a gift from him. The youth he chose could not refuse without admitting defeat at the outset, and he was compelled to cap the gift with an equal amount of property. When the time came for repayment if he had not doubled the original gift to return as interest, he was shamed and demoted, and his rival's prestige correspondingly enhanced.[22]

[22] Ibid., pp. 168-69.

And further on Benedict concludes:

> All the motivations they recognized centered around the will to superiority. Their social organization, their economic institutions, their religion, birth and death, were all channels for its expression. As they understood triumph, it involved ridicule and scorn heaped publicly upon one's opponents, who were, according to their customs, also their invited guests.[23]

Note in this passage that as an anthropologist, Benedict has used and also implied certain concepts to categorize Kwakiutl life. These concepts —institutions, role, status—serve to carve out and label various segments of tribal life. These concepts are objective and readily used by others wishing to describe the Kwakiutls, but beneath these objective and general categories are the particular behaviors governed by unique cultural perspectives and purposes. Objective social science concepts are very useful in getting at the unique rationales found in various cultures. But it is the unique configurations that are in need of explanation and a rational reconstruction provides that explanation.

In the case of the Kwakiutls, it is only when the full implications of their cultural rationale have been spelled out that it is possible to offer explanations for behaviors that to us appear baffling and even bizarre, for example, the seemingly rude and almost unimaginable treatment of their guests. During the Kwakiutl potlatches the host would display mocking life-sized figures of his guests. The posture of these carvings was unflattering, ribs protruding to symbolize poverty, and the host would proceed to sing of the insignificance of his guests. There were also songs celebrating the host, and the themes told of undiminished glories that in our culture would signify a rampant megalomania.

But the behavior of the Kwatkiutls makes sense in view of the purposes, desires, needs, and intentions created for the individual by the culture. Ridiculing one's guest is the thing to do. There are many good cultural reasons for doing so. Kwakiutl behavior is rational in the sense that it is consistent with rules and conventions of its culture that have helped formulate the purposes of the individuals acting in that culture. Benedict feels that behavior is explained when it can be judged appropriate for the context in which it is found.

Sociology is closely akin to anthropology in certain conceptual respects. The sociologist has the job of describing and explaining our social behavior, and he sets his task to make clear those conventions which though sometimes familiar are not perceived in all their ramifications. The sociologist is able to trace the unintended as well as the intended consequences of people's actions. Thus, for example, Max Weber's protestant

---

[23] Ibid., p. 171.

ethic thesis is an attempt to explain the development of capitalism as an unintended consequence of people holding a set of religious beliefs. Weber's thesis is aimed at showing that certain religious beliefs made it possible for people to justify as appropriate behavior a set of practices that led to the rise of capitalism. Certain protestant beliefs had the effect of causing people to take roles, establish conventions, and invent institutions that promoted the development of capitalism. In other words, the protestant ethic permitted people to assess capitalist behavior as the thing they should do. The explanatory force of Weber's thesis is in seeing the way in which protestantism and capitalism were linked.

It is important to note that in the explanation developed by Weber there is an attempt to link perceived intentions to unperceived effects. People did not explicitly say to themselves, "I hold certain beliefs and values because of my religion, and that permits me to be a capitalist." Rather, economic activities were a byproduct of actions aimed at other goals. In this case, Weber explains these by-products by showing them to be the result of actions calculated to produce other results. Thus unintended consequences are explained by rational reconstruction in the same way as intended consequences.

If sociologists are to show how social actions are justified, they must observe the behavior that actually occurs, use concepts to describe it, and present their descriptions in such a way that the justifying grounds behind the behavior can be understood. Many behaviors are so ordinary and easily understood that little explication of them is necessary. For instance, it is generally recognized what a handshake is and why people use it. But for the many behaviors that are obvious there are many that are not. They are masked in the apparently normal activities of the culture. Some conventions are subtle and people perform them without making explicit to others why they act as they do. William H. Whyte's *The Organization Man* is a description of a sociological phenomenon stemming from a complex set of roles characteristic of the managerial class in this country. Except for those playing the game within an organization, the behavior of managerial types will seem mysterious or even go unnoticed. It is only through careful empirical research that the unfamiliar and informal rules guiding the organization man can be discovered. In general, sociological inquiry is able to explain by making clear the rules and rationales that guide people's actions.

What, then, is the function of social science research that produces concepts and generalizations about human behavior. If the great bulk of the generalizations are not law-like, and this seems to be the case, then what value do they have? The authors contend that the basic function of these logical and empirical constructs is to serve as umbrellas under which specific actions can be placed in order to facilitate the task of offering rational explanations. Various concepts (role and status) and observed but non-law-like regularities (blue collar workers tend to vote Democratic) provide starting points in the process of assessing behavior. In other words, why is it that blue collar workers vote Democratic? What are their reasons?

Generalizations from the social sciences are frequently much more useful as something to be *explained* than they are as regularities that *explain* more specific behaviors and events. Observed regularities in society are often in need of explanation, and a satisfying way to do this is to offer a reconstruction of thought whether it be for an individual or an entire group. In suggesting that generalizations serve as something to be explained and as a starting point for rational explanations, we are turning generalizations on end when compared with their function in the science model of explanation.

By seeing concepts and generalizations in the social sciences as starting points in the process of rational explanation, social science takes on both objective and subjective dimensions. In using the concepts of his discipline to categorize phenomena, the researcher can operate objectively. In developing synthetic generalizations based on these concepts, he is offering publicly verifiable observations that are in principle objective products. However, in moving beyond concepts, generalizations, and empirical data to offer a rational assessment, the social scientist enters the subjective domain just as the historian. This part of the social scientist's task is similar to the historian's job of constructing a narrative. The social scientist (or ordinary citizen) tries to tell what is happening and what the significance of it all is in terms of human purpose. It is simply a fact of life that people will disagree over this because there are no objective standards with which to settle these disagreements.

One of the problems faced in developing explanations for human behavior is that people's perceptions and purposes change. Behavior is complex, not easily classified, and people frequently have a number of roles to fulfill. Frequently these roles are competing and incompatible. Thus someone's role as a corporation executive, elder in a church, and father may impose competing demands. Behavior is often a compromise of what is appropriate for each role, and behavior that is inappropriate for one role may be appropriate for another. Nor are rational explanations easy to develop for unintended consequences. It is no mean task to discover the relationship between seemingly disparate phenomena. To demonstrate that perceptions, purposes, and intentions in one area have an impact on an apparently unrelated phenomenon is one of the most significant tasks of the social sciences.

Implications for Curriculum

The primary curricular implication growing out of the arguments presented in this chapter is this: To the extent one believes that people need to know how to put events together in coherent narratives, and to the extent people should learn how to engage in a rational assessment of human behavior, the alternatives presented can serve as a basis for developing social studies curriculum. It would seem that the skill of being able to look at some data or analyze a set of experiences in terms of what happened, in the order it happened, and make judgments about the significance of it is something students at every grade level ought to develop. It involves skills of observation, classification, description, and evaluation, and these would seem to be relatively important and non-controversial among educational objectives. The skills involved in developing rational explanations are similar but involve a more complex level of reasoning and evaluation. There is some empirical evidence to indicate that explanations of this type should be dealt with primarily by junior and senior high students.[24] In general, however, it is up to the teacher to decide how successful he is in terms of getting students to understand the perspective of other people.

The rational explanation should be a strategy for getting students to learn what goes on inside another person's head. It is undoubtedly important for people to clarify their subjective picture of the world and their own values, but it is also important for them to come to an intimate understanding of other people's unique views of the world. It is important to the extent that one assumes that young people need to be sensitive to other conceptions of the world in order to deal effectively in a complex society and to be a good citizen. Rational explanations require a systematic, sympathetic, and accurate search for human motivation. This is a humanistic approach which requires one to understand other people in other times and circumstances. This kind of understanding comes with attempts to provide rational explanations.

It has been traditional with history curricula to claim that in studying the past, one gains an appreciation of it. Social science courses have frequently promised to offer insights into the nature of human behavior. Each may, of course, succeed in doing exactly what it claims, but if students do not have opportunities to engage in the kind of inquiry that produces rational explanations, there will be a lack of experience in a

24 E. A. Peel, "Some Problems in the Psychology of History Teaching" in W. H. Burston and D. Thompson, eds., *Studies in the Nature and Teaching of History* (New York: Humanities Press, Inc., 1967).

fundamental mode of explanation. It is fundamental not only because professional historians and social scientists use it, but also because it is frequently used in the daily lives of people in attempts to deal with the world about them.

In the ordinary conduct of human affairs people frequently want to explain behavior in terms of purpose and intention. The ordinary citizen is not usually prepared or inclined to play the role of social scientist as implied in scientific explanation. By necessity he makes decisions and takes positions in a style compatible with rational explanation. In a society of constant human interaction, we are all required to assess other people's behavior from time to time in order to govern our own. Whether it be a problem of understanding the employer's point of view, or understanding the Black Panthers' actions, the rational conception is a useful approach to explanation.

A curriculum that stresses the scrutinizing of other people's perspectives should effect less superficial judgments and generalizations about complex human interaction. In short, rational explanation is a way of providing students with practice in seeing other points of view, a practical as well as intellectual exercise. In a sense it is a model of value analysis. Its focus is frequently on people's values, and it can serve as a means of finding the possible and alternative value positions there are in the world. This is important because some curricula are designed to have students clarify their own values, or to take a stand on some controversial issue. It is true that some students have definite values and stands, but it is also true that many students do not even have a sense of the choices available. The rational reconstruction approach can provide students with an opportunity to see the various positions individuals, groups, or whole cultures have taken. Having other positions available provides a comparative base for building one's own values.

At this point it might be helpful to indicate at least briefly what curriculum materials might be like if they were based on this kind of explanation. First, the students would need to raise questions that were requests for rational explanations, seeking to understand the perspective of the actor in a situation. Such questions arise most easily out of specific contexts. Thus, a case study of a German citizen's reaction to the persecution of Jews during the 1930s could easily bring the question, "Why did Hans not object to this treatment of Jews?" This in turn could lead to a more general explanatory question concerning German culture and why there tended to be a society that passively accepted certain political actions. The goal would not be to make moral judgments about the German people, but rather to understand the social context the way they did. This approach would, of course, emphasize depth of treatment as opposed to covering a large amount of material.

For those interested in developing a more unconventional curriculum, there is no need to be tied to the usual subjects and disciplines. A teacher might wish to develop scenarios from futuristic societies. Students could be confronted with cases depicting life in the year 2500. (There is enough futuristic speculation and science fiction literature that there should be no problem getting ideas on what man and society might become.) Characters, events, and conditions could be presented to suggest roles and values different from what is now typical in our society. Students should explain events and actions and thereby come to understand the dominant values of the society. In other words, what would be the cultural context for human behavior in that society in the year 2500? How does it compare with our contemporary society?

It should be obvious that any explanatory question can be answered in more or less depth with more or less sophistication. The grade and interest level as well as the amount of time and materials available all bear upon the results of this kind of inquiry. But it should be noted that this conception assumes a depth of treatment not always found in curriculum. A serious question is whether students (and teachers) can engage in the kind of sustained effort required to develop reasonably adequate rational explanations.

Summary

It has been our intention in this chapter to suggest an alternative model around which social studies curriculum can be developed. We believe rational explanation and the narrative form can complement scientific explanation and the deductive form in establishing a balanced perspective in social studies curriculum.

Summary and Conclusions

7

Summary

The central theme of this book is that knowledge within the area of social studies should be derived from both subjective and objective perspectives. Justification for including both frames of reference rests on the belief that within the process of making social decisions in a democratic society, individual as well as group perspectives need to be considered. Thus as a part of our theme we suggest that a social studies curriculum ought to provide content and experiences that enable students to become sensitive to the riches existing in a variety of individual outlooks as well as to become socialized to commonly held, objective perspectives.

More concretely, we are asserting that social studies curriculum rather than swinging back and forth like a pendulum from objective to subjective emphases ought to include both. Some concepts, generalizations, and explanations within a social studies program ought to grow out of unique perspectives. Other such units of knowledge should be derived from particular disciplines or fields of study.

In addition to providing content and experiences from both subjective and objective points of view, a social studies program ought to permit students to become aware that both subjective and objective knowledge are legitimate aspects of social reality, and that this awareness is a prerequisite for making broad policy decisions. As social policy decisions are made, two questions must be kept in mind: (1) When should one be mindful of unique or subjective points of view? (2) When should one focus on commonly held or objective frames of reference?

These are basic questions around which a social studies curriculum ought to be constructed. The subjective-objective dimension on which they rest should be prominently emphasized throughout all levels of a social studies program. That is, content and experiences at the elementary and secondary levels should allow young people to see the legitimacy of personally-unique as well as commonly-held concepts, generalizations, and explanations and then to focus upon developing criteria for determining when it is most appropriate to devote attention to one or the other of the two kinds of knowledge. In addition to developing such criteria, students should also be led to understand the process of intelligently applying the criteria to life situations.

Students must also learn that the role of a person in helping others develop subjective knowledge is different from that of a person facilitating the development of objective knowledge. The role of a person fostering the development of subjective knowledge is that of a clarifier. In this role one may ask such questions as, "Are you saying that . . . ," "What do you mean by . . . ," "How did you come to decide that . . . ," "Do you feel that you are happy with . . . ," and "Would you be willing to act on . . . ." At no time should the clarifier attempt to force on another person concepts, generalizations, explanations, or evaluative criteria from some objective body of knowledge or from his unique perspective. Instead, his role should be that of a nondirective counselor.

On the other hand, the role of a person facilitating the development of objective knowledge is that of a representative or promoter of objectivity. He sees to it that concepts, generalizations, explanations, evaluative criteria, and methodology commonly held by scholars within a discipline or area of study are validly understood by others. In addition, he helps structure situations so that a group develops knowledge consistent with accepted standards of objectivity. Thus the role of a representative or promoter of objectivity requires one to understand the substance and methodology of various objective areas of study.

Teachers, as well as students, should understand that they have a responsibility to foster subjective and objective knowledge. At times a teacher will be a clarifier of subjective perspectives and at other times a representative or promoter of objective points of view. In order to know which of the two roles to take, he must be sensitive to the subjective and objective dimensions within the content and experiences he provides for students. For example, some social studies classes have conducted sensitivity or human relations sessions. The purpose of these sessions has been to open communication to become aware of the perspectives of others and to understand oneself as others see him. In these sessions, a teacher should see that becoming aware of the unique perspectives of others requires a clarification of various subjective frames of reference while coming to understand oneself as others see him requires the promotion of objective knowledge. The role of a teacher will vary according to the specific activities within these sessions.

While it is useful to separate the two roles of clarifier and representative or promoter, in practice they can be combined to complement each other within a particular context. For example, a teacher may ask a student, "How do you feel about blacks living in your neighborhood?" After hearing the students' reply, the teacher might switch to questions that get at objective knowledge to see how the student accommodates the information. Thus, after hearing negative feelings expressed about blacks, the teacher might interject information from anthropology: "Do you know that anthropologists are unable to find any evidence to indicate there are inferior races?" How does the student feel with objective knowledge like this? Clearly his unique feelings and attitudes are very significant in terms of how he responds to the race issue. However, on important social issues individuals are obligated to respond to (although not to accept) objective knowledge. Likewise a teacher has the obligation to confront students with objective as well as subjective perspectives on significant social issues.

Conclusions

We have attempted in this book to clarify meaning for three logical components of knowledge: *concept, generalization,* and *explanation.* We have focused on these three units because they constitute the basic logical elements of subjective and objective knowledge. Additionally we have asserted the legitimacy of both subjective and objective perspectives within a social studies curriculum.

In view of the analysis of concepts, generalizations and explanations, the authors wish to offer a number of conclusions about the development of a curriculum that deals effectively with both subjective and objective perspectives of these logical elements. In Chapters 4 and 5, it was suggested that it is quite difficult to develop generalizations and explanations of human events necessary to produce objective knowledge sought by those operating within the science model. Such generalizations tend to be non-law-like, and hence subject to change. In Chapter 6 an alternative view was offered in the form of the narrative model and rational explanation. The authors believe that the science model (deductive scientific explanations) is in and of itself an inadequate model on which to develop social studies curriculum, and that the alternative view offers an additional and viable approach to the development of curriculum that is both subjective and objective in perspective.

In advocating the narrative form and rational explanation as a model for constructing social studies curriculum, we are suggesting that it complement rather than exclude the science model. Social science generalizations tend to be non-law-like. As a result, they usually provide something less than adequate scientific explanations and predictions. Such generalizations do, however, permit one to be mindful of certain very abstract relationships that probably exist. Thus they can serve as orienting guides.

It is somewhat helpful, for example, to be aware of the following generalization if one wants to intelligently produce change within the context of a foreign culture:

> Those from another culture who try to introduce change may fail because they fail to understand how the people of the country perceive certain things.[1]

The generalization orients a person to be cognizant of the perspectives of those within the foreign culture, but it provides little guidance for making particular changes.

What one needs in this context is to have a storehouse of knowledge about possible perceptions, values, feelings, and purposes of people in a specific culture so he can interpret the particular cultural situation in which he finds himself. Even to know non-law-like generalizations about the perspectives within a particular culture is not enough if one happens to be dealing with an atypical individual or subgroup of that culture. Thus, generalizations from the social sciences serve primarily as orienting guides to intelligent behavior.

Since human behavior is purposive and somewhat irregular, what is needed in a social studies curriculum is a strong emphasis on understanding a wide array of human purposes as they relate to various actions

---

[1] Project Social Studies Center, University of Minnesota, *Resource Unit: Africa South of the Sahara*, p. 74.

or events. The narrative model and rational explanation seem to the authors to be fruitful vehicles for developing a curriculum that is relevant to this need. A curriculum could be quite broad to account for perceptions, purposes, values, and feelings of persons contributing to human events in a variety of contexts. First, in the ordinary affairs of daily life people easily and naturally develop narrative accounts to reconstruct the reasons for people's actions. Second, the work of some historians is conceived in these terms. For these scholars, to explain an event is to get under the skin of an historical agent, to reason and think as an actor thought within an event. Third, some social scientists are interested in developing rational accounts for social behavior. In doing so, they attempt to draw on purposes of people to account for the knowledge they produce.

Since the narrative model and rational explanation are applicable to past and present as well as to individual and general human events, one is not committed to any particular discipline or area of inquiry in building a curriculum. Included in a curriculum might be rational accounts for broad generalizations, for more limited kinds of generalizations, and for unique, individual events. What we are saying is that a curriculum consciously based on rational explanation would be a balanced curriculum in that it could use historical or social science concepts and generalizations. It could be used in nondisciplinary or ordinary affairs encountered by the general citizenry. It meets the challenge of those who criticize the "new social studies" as too abstract, irrelevant, and neglectful of humanistic problems.

An intended outcome of any curriculum based on rational explanation would be to provide abundant opportunity for making students more sensitive to the subtleties of the human personality. The emphasis on perceiving other people's values would presumably lead them out of their own unique perspectives and peer culture. It should provide young people with examples of alternative values and cultural perspectives and thereby broaden their understanding of human nature. Within this kind of curriculum, then, students would focus on various possible subjective perspectives, and they would also gain experience within an objective frame of reference as they used inquiry procedures to validate views of particular persons or groups.

Rational explanation could provide opportunities for students to clarify their own values as they worked through various explanatory situations. For example, after developing an account of why a particular person or group acted as they did, students could present their own views on what the appropriate action in a given context should have been. In other words, students could be asked, "Based on your own purposes, perspectives, and values, how would you have acted in that situation?" This kind of exercise forces a person to state his assumptions, means, and ends. Questions can be raised about the consistency of a person's values, or the congruence between his means and ends, or the morality of his value position.[2]

Finally, a curriculum emphasizing rational explanation looks at human behavior in terms of human responsibility for that behavior. The authors believe that this is an important by-product of this approach. We do not intend to argue that individuals are solely responsible for what they do, nor are we arguing that because people have good reasons for their actions they have not been manipulated by external forces. The whole question of the various forms and degrees of responsibility for particular actions is a difficult one that we have not attempted to deal with in this book. However, we do contend that human behavior is basically purposive and that it is important for people to consciously look for the purposes that motivate actions. Certainly it is both useful and essential to frequently look at broad social forces acting upon human beings to gain a perspective on the society as a whole. But behind broad socially descriptive categories (such as technology or racism) are people who are affected in terms of how they perceive the world—both in terms of their factual understanding of the world and the values they hold. We believe it is most useful for young people to understand, for example, the impact of technology—how it affects people's purposes and consequent actions. In other words, broad social forces should be studied in terms of how they affect people who continue to be responsible for their own behavior. There should be an emphasis on making people consciously reflective on why they act as they do and on bringing out the unintended as well as intended consequences.

To conclude, the authors wish to point out that while there are few formal curriculum materials available that ask students to develop narratives and engage in rational explanation, it is well within the means of most teachers to develop their own materials. Certain historical situations lend themselves to this approach. There is much in the way of anthropology, sociology, and political science which could be adapted. Many contemporary situations could be developed to fit this approach. It was suggested in the preceding chapter that futuristic materials—novels like *Brave New World*—could be used to focus on the explanatory analysis of behavior. Students might fruitfully analyze the nature of their so-

---

[2] This approach of getting students to justify their own position on an issue is a basic component of the Harvard Social Studies Project which has been developed into the Public Issues series by Donald Oliver and Fred M. Newmann and published by American Education Publications, Columbus, Ohio. This approach to curriculum focuses on asking a person to answer the question, "What would you have done in that situation?" The person is then forced to justify his actions.

ciety in terms of the purposes and values people have and how it affects their behavior.

What we have attempted to offer in this book is a particular kind of analysis that will stimulate the development of a comprehensive, consistent, and thoughtful social studies curriculum—one that meets the needs of individuals and of society.

Index

Factual statements, 26
Fact-value continuum, 39-40
Family instability, 53
Farmers, 84
Fenton, Edwin, 7-8, 44n, 52
Forecasting election trends, 68
Frame of reference, 7
Framework and objectivity, 96-97
Frequency generalizations, 64
Frontier and democracy, 84
Frustration, 69-70
"Function of General Laws in History, The" (Hempel), 80
Function of generalizations, 52-56

G

Galileo, 69
General propositions, *see* Generalizations
Generalizations, 6-8, 10-11, 51-71, 118-19
  characteristics of, 56-59
    conditional claims as, 57-58
    necessary or substitutable conditions as, 58
    quantification claims as, 57-58
    reversible or irreversible claims as, 57-58
  as statement, 56-58
    sufficient or contingent conditions as, 58
  curriculum and, 70-71
  law-like, 62-64, 78-79, 84-85, 87, 89, 100, 106
  laws, theories and, 64-66
  role and function of, 52-56
  social science laws and, 66-70
  synthetic and analytic, 34, 59-62
Generalizing abstractions as concepts, 19-28, 31-33
Genetics, 77
Geography taught in junior high schools, 4
Goal-directed behavior, 104
Goodnow, Jacqueline, 17n
Gottschalk, Louis, 107n
Goudge, T. A., 99n
Gravity, 62

H

Hanna, Paul, 7-8
Harmin, Merrill, 41n, 44-45
Harvard "jurisprudential" curriculum, 45-46
Health, 4
Hempel, Carl, 65, 75-76, 77n, 80-82, 95
Henderson, Kenneth B., 22, 36n

Hickman, Warren, 21n
High School Geography project, 25
History:
  rational explanations in, 99-107
  scientific explanations in, 80-84
  as trend in social science curriculum, 3
Holt Social Studies Course, 44
Homans, George, 53, 60, 66, 68, 70, 77
Hullfish, H. Gordon, 28-30
Hunt, Earl B., 22
Hunt, Maurice P., 38-39, 46-47, 52
Hypothesis, 7

I

Ideas as concepts, 17-18
Ideology, 7
Inquiry-centered learning, 52
Integrationists, 47
Intergenerational mobility, 53
Irreversible claims, 57-58

J

Junior High Schools, 4

K

K-12 curriculum, 6
Kasperson, Roger E., 26n
Knowledge, components of, 10-14, 117-18
Kuhn, Thomas, 12, 92n
Kwakiutl Indians, 109-10

L

Law-like generalizations, 62-64, 78-79, 84-85, 87, 89, 100, 106
Laws, 63, 70
  generalizations and, 64-66
  social science, 66-70
Leadership, 7
Lee, John R., 7n
Leisure, worthy use of, 4
Leonard, Henry S., 36n
Louch, A. R., 108n
Lower class, family instability in, 53

M

Marin, Janet, 22
Martin, Jane R., 3n, 72-73
Marx, Karl, 42
Massialas, Byron, 52, 63n
Meeting needs of society as trend in social science curriculum, 4